Corey,

Congratulations on your High School Graduation. We are so proud of you!

Like a Zeppelin filled with helium, here's knowing it will take you soaring to new heights on your life's journey. We love you!!!!

Love, Mom & Dad

Led Zeppelin
The Illustrated Biography

Led Zeppelin
The Illustrated Biography

GARETH THOMAS

Published by Transatlantic Press
First published in 2009
This edition published 2011

Transatlantic Press
38 Copthorne Road, Croxley Green, Hertfordshire, WD3 4AQ

For photograph copyrights see page 224

A catalogue record for this book is available from the British Library.
ISBN 978-1-907176-25-8

Printed and bound in China

Contents

Introduction

When Jimmy Page, Robert Plant, John Paul Jones and John "Bonzo" Bonham first gathered in a London rehearsal space in late 1968, few could have predicted that within just five years they would be piloting the biggest band in the world towards an almost unprecedented level of success. Perhaps fewer still could have foreseen their enduring appeal and impact, but with a combination of raw talent, dogged determination and the fanatical support of audiences around the globe, Led Zeppelin would transcend their relatively inauspicious beginnings to establish themselves as one of the most important and influential bands in the history of rock and roll.

Although initially guided by Page, who had assembled the group in the wake of the Yardbirds' demise, Led Zeppelin quickly developed a distinctive sound that combined the practiced musicianship of former session musicians Page and Jones with the unbridled passion of Plant and Bonham. While rooted in the blues, their music would fuse elements of folk, country, soul, funk and reggae, as well as Middle Eastern, Asian and African influences. Characterized by Plant's urgent, soulful wail, Page's heavy riffs and virtuoso solo work, Jones' melodic, driving bass and atmospheric keyboards, and Bonham's power and dexterity, Led Zeppelin's music would effectively come to define the sound of hard rock in the 1970s – perfectly embodying a contrast between delicacy and weight.

However, this dynamic between light and shade would find a mirror in the extreme highs and lows of Led Zeppelin's career, for their extreme success would be tainted by rumours of drug addiction, debauchery and even ritual magic, whilst the band's later years would be touched by personal tragedy, such as Robert Plant's serious injury in a car accident in 1975, the loss of his young son just two years later and the tragic death of John Bonham in 1980, which finally led to the group's decision to disband.

Through a combination of stunning photographs and insightful captions, this book chronicles the meteoric rise to fame of one of the world's biggest bands, from their roots in the British Blues scene, through the highs and lows of relentless touring, and the success and excesses of stardom, to assume their rightful place in the pantheon of rock and roll. Furthermore, it charts the solo projects, collaborations and reunions that have taken place since Led Zeppelin's official demise in 1980, including the band's triumphant and long awaited return to the stage in 2007.

From their earliest days, to their position as one of the most successful groups of all time, Led Zeppelin's uncompromising attitude, dynamism and innovation have set them apart as true pioneers, who have forged an enduring legacy that continues to influence and inspire new generations of musicians and fans to this day.

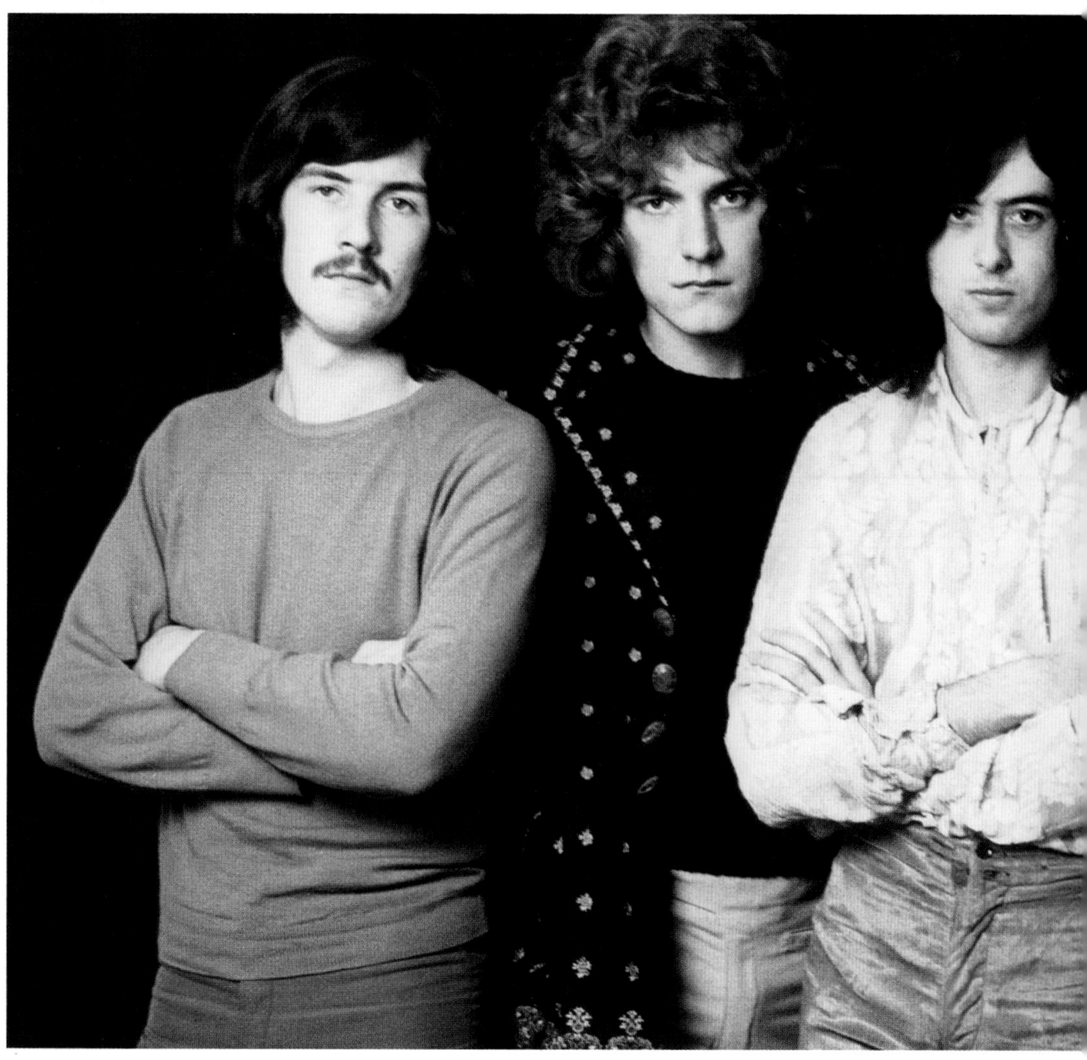

Part One

Dazed and Confused

Talented guitarist

Opposite: Jimmy Page in 1965. Page acquired his first guitar at the age of 13 in 1957 and aged 14 he appeared on a televised talent show. By 1961 he was performing professionally with Neil Christian and the Crusaders, making his debut recording on their single "The Road To Love". After a bout of glandular fever, Jimmy quit touring and enrolled at art college in Sutton, but he was soon back on stage and back in the studio, becoming a sought-after session musician. During the early 1960s "Little Jimmy Page" laid down tracks for such artists as the Kinks, The Nashville Teens, Them, Tom Jones and The Who.

Above: Having previously turned down an invitation to replace Eric Clapton in the Yardbirds – instead recommending his friend Jeff Beck – Jimmy relented in June 1966, initially taking up the bass, before joining Beck on lead guitar duties. However, within a matter of months Beck had quit the group, and by early 1968, against a backdrop of increasing commercial pressure and growing musical differences, the Yardbirds were beginning to fall apart.

Band of Joy

Opposite: Page during his Yardbirds days. Even as the Yardbirds started to fracture, Page considered reviving the group with new personnel. While he had been carving out his reputation in London as a "hip young guitar slinger", John Paul Jones had been making a name for himself as a bassist and session arranger, albeit with rather less fanfare. Hearing of Jimmy's possible new venture, Jones let it be known that his services were available. Their professional paths having already crossed on more than one occasion, Page was aware of Jones' considerable skill; however, a question remained as to where he might find a suitably talented vocalist and drummer.

Above: The Band of Joy in 1968 (with Robert Plant and John Bonham second and third from left). Having approached singer Terry Reid, Page was pointed in the direction of one Robert Plant, a relative unknown from Staffordshire, who had recently struck up an association with "The Father of British Blues", Alexis Korner. Prior to this, Plant had spent years plugging away with various bands on the Midlands blues and soul scene, perhaps most notably with the Band of Joy, whose shifting line-up ultimately included a notoriously powerful drummer called John Henry Bonham.

Completing the line up

Opposite and right: Early promo shots of the New Yardbirds. Having been to see Robert Plant performing with the band Hobstweedle near Birmingham, Jimmy Page invited him to spend a few days at his riverside home in Pangbourne, Berkshire. They listened to music and discussed plans for the new band, with Plant recommending his former band-mate John Bonham for the role of drummer. However, with steady work backing Tim Rose and offers on the table from Chris Farlowe and Joe Cocker, Bonham took a little convincing. He was also concerned that the Yardbirds were a dead entity, particularly in Britain, but eventually Page and Plant talked him round, and by August the line-up was complete.

Later that month, Page, Plant, Jones and Bonham assembled in a basement studio in London for their first rehearsal. It was the first time that Plant and Bonham had met Jones, and all of them were understandably tentative, but their fears were instantly allayed by the musical chemistry between them. This was just as well, as within a matter of days the group would be heading to Scandinavia, for Jimmy Page and manager Peter Grant had not only inherited the rights to the Yardbirds' name, but also their remaining contractual obligations.

Debut performance

Opposite and above: On 7 September 1968, the band made their debut performance in Gladsaxe, Denmark. It was the first of two shows that night – the second being in nearby Brondby – launching a week-long tour of Denmark and Sweden, during which the band would be variously billed as the Yardbirds, and the Yardbirds featuring Jimmy Page. Taking their cue from the first rehearsal, the sets for these shows incorporated a number of Yardbirds' staples, such as "Train Kept a Rolling", and "Dazed and Confused", which included Jimmy's use of a violin bow on his guitar strings, as well as the Band of Joy favourite "As Long As I Have You" by Garnett Mimms. However, even at this early stage a distinctive sound was beginning to emerge, which united the studied musicianship of Page and Jones with the raw, unpolished power of Plant's vocals and Bonham's thunderous drum attack.

From Yardbirds to Led Zeppelin

Right: Returning to Britain in mid-September, it was evident that the group required a new name to differentiate themselves from the Yardbirds of old. Not only had they already begun to move in new and exciting directions, but there remained the possibility of a legal challenge from former Yardbirds bassist Chris Dreja, who also still had rights to the name. Remembering a conversation with Keith Moon and John Entwhistle of The Who, with whom Page had considered forming a supergroup two years earlier, Jimmy proffered "Lead Zeppelin" – a reference to "going down like a lead balloon" – and the name stuck, with a slight change of spelling to avoid any possible mispronunciation. Towards the end of the month, Led Zeppelin entered the studio to make some initial recordings, before embarking on a series of British club and university dates, their first as Led Zeppelin taking place at Surrey University on 25 October. The following month, recording of the band's eponymous debut album was completed in London, and just days before Christmas 1968, they jetted off to the US, to begin their first North American tour on Boxing Day, at the Denver Coliseum, Colorado.

Success in the US

Opposite: Jones seen during a recording for Danish television in Copenhagen, March 1969. By the time the first North American tour drew to a close in Miami in mid-February, Led Zeppelin had already made quite an impression on US audiences, with a series of triumphant performances in Hollywood, San Francisco, Boston and New York. However, their debut album, which had been released in the States in January, had been rather less well received by most of the press, who seemed to regard it as derivative and formulaic. Nevertheless, the band were keen to maintain their momentum, embarking on a series of British and European dates from 1 March to mid-April, during which time they would return to Sweden and Denmark, and record their first sessions for the BBC.

Right: On 18 April, just days after completing their UK outing, the band touched down in the US to begin their second North American tour at the New York University Jazz Festival.

Debut album makes US top 10

Opposite and above: Led Zeppelin passing through a US airport during their second trip to America. Having launched the tour in New York, it was on to San Francisco for four nights, taking in both the Winterland Ballroom and the Fillmore West, with support from Julie Driscoll, Brian Auger and the Trinity, as well as the Coldwell-Winfield Blues Band. "Whole Lotta Love" received its live debut at the Winterland on 26 April, and new material was developed both on and off-stage. The tour was punctuated by a number of studio sessions in New York, Los Angeles and Vancouver, with the aim of completing a second album in time for summer release.

By May, the band's debut LP, *Led Zeppelin*, had entered the US top ten, and as their popularity continued to grow, so too did their confidence. It had been less than six months since their first American shows and yet Led Zeppelin were already beginning to share the top billing at venues that were sold out.

Hell-raisers

Above: John Bonham in rehearsals during the second US tour. As the tour progressed through California and then north to Canada and Seattle, Led Zeppelin were not only developing a reputation for their blistering live performances, but also for destruction and debauchery, with hotel rooms being trashed and rumours circulating about lewd acts with groupies. With the exception of Jimmy Page, each member of the group was now married with children, but the combination of boredom, loneliness and post-performance adrenaline would lead them all to indulge themselves, and alongside tour manager Richard Cole, Bonham in particular gained a reputation for hell-raising.

Opposite: John Paul Jones with photographer Charles Bonnay. Although Jones was not indifferent to the excesses of life on the road, he had a tendency to maintain a lower profile than his bandmates, preferring to escape his hotel room when possible or take in the local sights.

Life on the road

Opposite and above: Page and Plant in the restaurant of a Howard Johnson's hotel. Despite all the high-jinx, life on the road for Led Zeppelin could be tough. They were frequently subject to ridicule and abuse on account of their long hair and flamboyant dress, and often complained that they had trouble getting served in restaurants. However, there were also darker experiences – the band even stumbled across a murder scene in the hotel lobby on arrival in Detroit.

In spite of the rapturous reception that they were receiving at gigs, Led Zeppelin also still had to contend with a largely hostile press, so when their entourage was joined in Detroit by *Life* magazine journalist Ellen Sander, Peter Grant encouraged his charges to behave themselves. Any opportunity for redemption was squandered when Sander refused to file her report, which was perhaps just as well, for while the band had found her aloof and hostile, she seemed to regard them as especially depraved.

Live with The Who

Opposite: Led Zeppelin live on the US East Coast in the spring of 1969. Following performances in Athens and Minneapolis, Zeppelin headed for two nights at Chicago's Kinetic Playground, on 23 and 24 May. They were also due to perform at the Northern California Folk-Rock Festival alongside the Jimi Hendrix Experience and Jefferson Airplane that weekend, but eventually opted not to appear. Instead, on 25 May, Led Zeppelin shared their one and only billing with fellow British rockers The Who, at the Merriweather Post Pavilion, Columbia, Maryland.

Right: Peter Grant takes Led Zeppelin on a shopping trip to a trendy House of Lewis store. The fashion outlet became as famous for its celebrity patronage as for the groundbreaking designs it produced, counting such stars as Zeppelin, Joe Cocker and the Rolling Stones amongst its clientele.

Grant was maintaining a fearsome reputation as a manager not to be messed with. Not only had he secured his band an unprecedented record deal with Atlantic Records, but he remained ever-alert to unscrupulous promoters and theatre owners.

Plant's distinctive vocal style

Opposite and above: If Plant and Bonham had felt themselves somewhat in Jimmy Page's shadow during the first American tour, they were by now starting to be recognized for their distinct personalities and musical contributions. Multiple encores aside, Led Zeppelin frequently closed their sets with an extensive drum solo from Bonham, during which he would jettison his drumsticks and play with his bare hands – often until they bled. Entitled "Pat's Delight" in honour of his wife, the solo provided Bonham with both a chance to let off some steam and a showcase for his formidable talent. Robert Plant meanwhile was rapidly becoming the star of the group. As the frontman this was perhaps to be expected, but Plant was not only developing his distinctive vocal style and command of the stage, but behind the scenes he was also beginning to develop a songwriting partnership with Page – notably supplying all of the lyrics for "Thank You".

Feeling the pressure

Opposite and above: Towards the end of the second North American tour, Led Zeppelin were beginning to feel the pressures engendered by their punishing schedule. After shows in Chicago and Maryland, the ever-frail Jimmy Page had come down with a bout of flu, while Plant, Jones and Bonham were by now desperately missing their families. Since their first gig in September 1968, the band had been almost permanently on the road, and Plant was feeling desperately guilty about the lack of time he had spent with his wife and baby daughter. Plant had married Maureen Wilson on 9 November, and that very night had taken to the stage with Led Zeppelin at London's Roundhouse, and their daughter, Carmen, had been born in the midst of the British tour, just weeks before the band had left for their first slog across the States.

TRANS WORLD
TRAN

Working on a second album

Opposite: Page, Plant and Jones in the foyer of the Boston Tea Party, May 1969. Despite the strain that was starting to show, there was little time for Led Zeppelin to relax or recuperate, besides which they would soon be on their way home. After Maryland, the group headed to Boston for three nights at the Tea Party, which were attended by numerous Atlantic Records' staff and where support came from Tommy Bolin's hard rock outfit Zephyr. Led Zeppelin were contracted to play for just 50 minutes, but already their sets were regularly lasting over an hour and a half, incorporating extended jam sessions and several encores, which typically included improvised medleys of blues standards, and occasional renditions of songs by the Beatles and Rolling Stones.

Above: Jimmy Page in a US recording studio in late May. As the tour neared its conclusion, Led Zeppelin were yet to complete work on their second album, but at the end of the month they were back in the studio, laying down such tracks as "What Is And What Should Never Be", "Heartbreaker" and "Ramble On".

IMPORTED
& Co's PALE ALE

Fillmore East

Opposite and above: Page and Bonham backstage at the Fillmore East, New York. The second North American tour concluded with four sold-out shows at the venue over two days, where support came from jazz legend Woody Herman, and the soul-rock revue Delaney & Bonnie and Friends, who would go on to find fame supporting Eric Clapton's supergroup, Blind Faith. However, it was the headline act that the audiences had come to see, and they were not disappointed, as Led Zeppelin treated them to a succession of searing performances. The sets opened with the old favourite "Train Kept a Rolling" and one gig included a medley of early rock and roll numbers such as Chuck Berry's "Roll Over Beethoven" and Jerry Lee Lewis' "Walk On Down The Line". The shows received detailed and positive reviews from some quarters, although as usual, major publications such as *Variety* magazine were less favourable, criticizing the band for a lack of subtlety and their reliance on high volume.

First gold disc

Left: Plant backstage at the Fillmore East. After the final show on 31 May, the boys were rewarded with a party at New York's Plaza hotel, at which they were to receive their first gold discs for sales of their debut album, *Led Zeppelin I*. However, as soon as the party was over, Page took Led Zeppelin into A&R Studios in New York to continue recording sessions for their forthcoming LP.

Opposite: A promotional shot taken in the US in May. By the time the band returned to Britain in June, word of Led Zeppelin's American success had filtered home, and rather than rest on their laurels, the band chose instead to embark on a series of British dates, beginning at Birmingham Town Hall on the 13th of the month, and taking in Manchester, Newcastle, Bristol and Preston. These dates were augmented by several radio sessions for the BBC and a trip to Paris to record for the French TV show *Tous En Scene*, as well as further recording sessions for the second album.

The Bath Festival of Blues

Opposite and above: Riding high on a wave of successful UK shows and some positive reviews in such publications as the *NME*, on 28 June 1969 Led Zeppelin took to the stage for their biggest British gig so far, performing for a crowd of some 12,000 people at the Bath Festival of Blues, on a bill that also featured Fleetwood Mac, John Mayall, Ten Years After, the Nice, and Roy Harper. Despite an afternoon slot and the constraints of a relatively short set, Zeppelin wowed the assembled masses – as they would the following night, closing their UK tour with a headlining appearance at the Royal Albert Hall, on the first night of the Pop Proms. Having overrun by some minutes, the band's electricity was briefly cut, and people began to leave the auditorium, but the power was restored after protests from Plant, to the delight of the remaining fans, who were treated to a rendition of Little Richard's "Long Tall Sally".

Newport Jazz Festival

Opposite: Led Zeppelin at the Newport Jazz Festival, Rhode Island. Having made their first real breakthrough on home turf, and with their debut album set to peak just outside the UK top five, Led Zeppelin turned their attention back to the US, launching their third North American tour at the massive Atlanta Pop Festival on 5 July. This was followed the next day by a headlining slot at the Newport Jazz Festival and, in addition to a host of smaller venues, the band appeared at numerous large outdoor events throughout July and August, including the Schaefer Music Festival in Central Park, the Mid-West Rock Festival and the Seattle Pop Festival. At the Singer Bowl Music Festival in New York Peter Grant had to manhandle a near-naked Bonham from the stage after he had joined the Jeff Beck Group for an impromptu jam session. At the same time, Jimmy Page completed the final mixing of *Led Zeppelin II*, and on 31 August the tour closed at the Texas International Pop Festival. Left: Page on stage in Bath.

One year on

Opposite and above: Led Zeppelin backstage at London's Lyceum Theatre. In September 1969, following a year of near-incessant touring, Led Zeppelin were finally given a well deserved break, with no performance or recording commitments for the entire month. Whilst Jimmy Page headed to Morocco and Spain with his girlfriend in tow, the others were able to retreat into the relative normality of family life. It was also a chance for the group to reflect and take stock of their achievements – it was little more than a year since they had assembled in London for their first rehearsal, and yet they had not only effectively conquered America, but had reached the top ten on both sides of the Atlantic with their debut album, with another in the can awaiting release. No sooner had October begun, than Zeppelin were back on the road attempting to hone a new set incorporating material from the long-awaited second LP, and following dates in Holland and Paris, Led Zeppelin convened at the Lyceum Theatre for a historic show.

Rocking Carnegie Hall

Opposite and right: Bonham and Jones at the Lyceum Theatre, London. On 12 October Led Zeppelin performed a showcase set at the Lyceum, which included previews of "Heartbreaker" and "What Is And What Should Never Be", for which they reportedly received their highest British fee thus far. Less than a week after the show, the band was once again back in America, launching their autumn tour at the prestigious Carnegie Hall – a venue that had not played host to a rock band since the Rolling Stones some five years earlier. The tour lasted until 8 November, by which time *Led Zeppelin II* had been released, and "Whole Lotta Love" had been issued in the US, where radio stations had already been airing an edited version. In the UK, however, Peter Grant pulled the single, refusing to capitulate to the demands of the record company and radio stations.

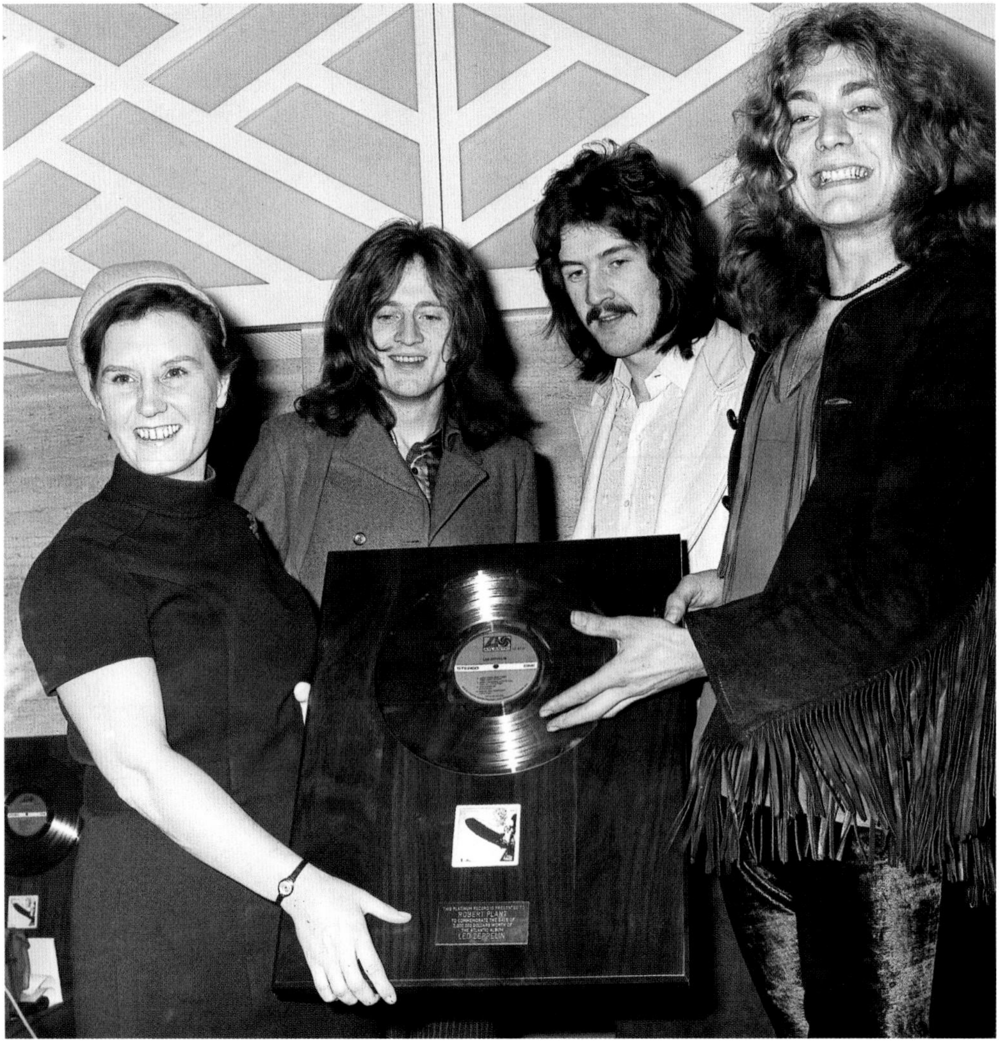
ROBERT PLANT
LED ZEPPELIN

Led Zeppelin II released

Opposite and right: On 11 December 1969 the group were presented with gold and platinum discs by Gwyneth Dunwoody, the Parliamentary Secretary to the Board of Trade at the Savoy Hotel, London. Page was unable to attend after receiving minor injuries in a car accident en route to the ceremony. With their platinum-selling debut album still on the US top 20, *Led Zeppelin II* was released on 22 October, and with the aid of massive advance orders, it turned gold within a week – soaring up the *Billboard* chart from 199th to 15th place. Three weeks later the album stalled at number two behind the Beatles' *Abbey Road*, but before the year was out it would claim the top spot, where it would remain for some seven weeks.

"The Nobs"

Above and opposite: John Bonham and Jimmy Page on stage in Copenhagen. In early 1970 the band had gone back on tour, playing a series of UK dates in January, before heading for Europe, and on 28 February they performed in Copenhagen as "the Nobs", having been threatened with legal action by Countess Eva Von Zeppelin. As 1970 began, "Whole Lotta Love" peaked at number four in the US charts, while *Led Zeppelin II* continued its climb to the top of the UK charts.

A tour beset with problems

Right: Robert Plant on stage in February 1970.

Opposite: A publicity picture of the band. In March 1970 Zeppelin launched their North American spring offensive in Vancouver. It would be their first tour without support, and they would play to some of their biggest audiences so far. Despite some memorable high points, however, the tour was beset with problems from start to finish, with Page's guitar disappearing en route to Canada, Peter Grant being threatened at gunpoint in Memphis, and Plant finally losing his voice ahead of the last show in Las Vegas. Back from the States in April, Page and Plant retreated to Bron-Yr-Aur cottage in Wales, in order to relax and write material for their next album. Keen to minimise exposure to the clinical conditions of the studio, by May recording had begun at Headley Grange, a stately home in Hampshire. As the summer progressed, Led Zeppelin somehow found time to play some live dates in Europe. This included a triumphant return to the Bath Festival as headliners. Held at the Bath and West Showground, Shepton Mallet, the festival attracted some 150,000 people, and marked something of a turning point for the band in Britain.

Madison Square Garden

Opposite and above: Page and Plant attend a press conference in New York, September 1970.

Following four consecutive nights in Germany in July, and further recording sessions that were held at the newly-opened Island Studios in London, Led Zeppelin launched their sixth North American tour at the Yale Bowl, New Haven, Connecticut on 15 August. The tour had originally been scheduled to begin ten days earlier in Cincinnati, Ohio, but several dates were cancelled after John Paul Jones' father suffered a bout of ill health. Despite this setback, once underway the tour would prove to be a major success, with the band now commanding a minimum of $25,000 a night, and on 19 September they grossed over $100,000 for their final two shows at New York's Madison Square Garden. However, Led Zeppelin's relationship with the US media remained strained, and the mutual suspicion was all too apparent at a press conference held ahead of the New York shows.

FARFISA

Multiple encores

Opposite and right: Plant and Page on stage at the LA Forum, 4 September 1970. Playing without any support acts, Led Zeppelin were now regularly performing sets in excess of two hours, which allowed them not only to incorporate some of the new material that they had written for their forth-coming third LP, but also to experiment with extended jam sessions and alternative arrangements. John Bonham's drum solos now frequently exceeded 15 minutes, while original compositions such as "Whole Lotta Love" and "Communication Breakdown" would often segue into a medley of blues and rock and roll standards, featuring such songs as John Lee Hooker's "Let That Boy Boogie", Hank Snow's "I'm Moving On", and the Beatles' "I Saw Her Standing There".

Acoustic sets

Above: Jimmy Page onstage at the LA Forum, 4 September 1970. During their sixth North American tour, Led Zeppelin typically opened their shows with the driving "Immigrant Song", a Viking battle-cry inspired in part by Zeppelin's visit to Iceland some months earlier. However, much of the new material that had been written for the third album was in a decidedly folksy, acoustic vein, which not only reflected the fact that many of the songs had originally emerged from the relaxed sessions at Bon-Yr-Aur, where there was no electricity, but also echoed Page and Plant's desire to evolve musically, and revealed a gentler, more introspective side to their writing. From this time onwards, the group began to incorporate an acoustic set into their live performances, whilst John Paul Jones increasingly made use of organ as well as bass guitar.

Opposite: John Paul Jones and Jimmy Page at the Forum.

Replacing the Beatles

Opposite: In mid-September, while Led Zeppelin were enjoying a short break in Hawaii, English music magazine *Melody Maker* had printed the results of its readers' poll, declaring "Zeppelin Topple Beatles". Robert Plant had been awarded Best British Male Vocalist, *Led Zeppelin II* had won Best British Album, and perhaps most notably, the band had ended the Beatles' eight year reign as Top Group. Returning to Britain from what was probably their most successful tour yet, the band collected their awards at a ceremony held in late September.

Right: The following month saw the release of *Led Zeppelin III*, which rapidly rose to the top of the charts in both the UK and US. Although the album's chart tenure would be relatively brief, with advance orders nearing 1 million in the US alone it sold in vast numbers. However, both Page and Plant were dismayed by critical reaction to the LP, for many of the publications that had previously derided the group for their brand of heavy rock were now accusing them of attempting to emulate the lighter sounds of bands such as Crosby, Stills and Nash.

Stairway To Heaven

Above: Led Zeppelin in a publicity shot circa 1970. Despite the mixed reception prompted by the release of their third album, as 1970 drew to a close Jimmy Page and Robert Plant returned to the Welsh rural idyll of Bron-Yr-Aur to resume songwriting. It was here that they began laying some of the foundations for what would perhaps prove to be their masterwork, an album that would encapsulate the vision of "light and shade" that Page had for so long been striving to achieve. Following the initial sessions in Wales, Page and Plant were once again reunited with Jones and Bonham at Headley Grange, where the new tracks started to take shape using the Rolling Stones' mobile studio. Amongst these was an epic composition that would evolve into one of rock's defining moments, "Stairway To Heaven".

Opposite: Currently immersing himself in the writings of Scottish folklorist Lewis Spence, Plant also crafted the lyrics for "The Battle of Evermore" at those same sessions, with Fairport Convention's Sandy Denny being brought in to share vocal duties.

Hertz
RIZED FOR
EUR SERVIC
RS ONLY

Part Two

Electric Magic

World's top band

Above: Led Zeppelin and Peter Grant (left) receive gold discs from Board of Trade official Anthony Grant (centre) towards the end of 1970. 1971 began well for Zeppelin – in January "Immigrant Song" peaked at number 16 on the US singles chart, and as recording sessions continued throughout February, Led Zeppelin were voted World's Top Band at the Disc and Music Echo awards in London. On 5 March, the band launched their "Back to the Clubs" tour at Ulster Hall in Belfast, where "Stairway to Heaven" received its live debut, with Page performing the song on his custom-built double-necked Gibson guitar. The tour ended at London's Marquee at the end of the month, and was followed in early April by a one off performance at the Paris Cinema in London, which was recorded for John Peel's *In Concert* radio show. During the summer, Led Zeppelin played a handful of European dates, which would include one of the band's lowest points, when full scale rioting erupted in Milan. This was largely attributed to the Italian police, who had begun firing tear gas to subdue rowdy elements in the crowd. The band were forced to abandon the stage, which was then overrun.

Opposite: Robert Plant on stage in London in 1971.

Seventh North American tour

Opposite and left: Robert Plant and Jimmy Page onstage at Madison Square Garden, New York, September 1971. Leaving behind the turmoil of Milan, Led Zeppelin arrived in Vancouver on 19 August to begin their seventh North American tour, with Plant celebrating his 23rd birthday that night. However the show was not without incident, as hundreds of ticketless fans attempted to force their way into the already overcrowded venue and some damage was caused to the stage. A partial stage collapse also occurred at Madison Square Garden on 3 September. While the band were pleased with the reaction to new material such as "Stairway to Heaven", "Black Dog" and "Rock and Roll", there were numerous scares during the tour, including death threats. As a result, Led Zeppelin became more reclusive, and holed up in their hotels between shows, where boredom would sometimes spill into destruction. Closing the tour in Hawaii, Zeppelin enjoyed a few days rest, before heading to Japan for shows in Tokyo, Hiroshima and Osaka. If Led Zeppelin were unprepared for the rapturous welcome that they received from Japanese audiences, then the Tokyo Hilton was similarly unprepared for Led Zeppelin, who were swiftly banned for life.

"Four symbols" tops UK chart

Opposite and right: Jimmy Page and Robert Plant on stage at the Wembley Empire Pool, November 1971. After Japan, Page and Plant spent some time in Hong Kong, Thailand and India, before returning to Britain in time for the release of their fourth album. The LP had originally been scheduled for release months earlier, but problems with its engineering, and then a protracted dispute with Atlantic Records over the sleeve art ensured it was long overdue. Page had insisted that the music be allowed to speak for itself, with no mention of the band's name on the cover, although he would be listed as producer, and Plant's lyrics for "Stairway..." would be printed inside. In addition, each member of the group had selected a symbol to represent them on the label, and while the album has no official title, it is often referred to as "four symbols", or "Zoso" after the symbol Page designed for himself. Days after the album's release, Led Zeppelin embarked on a series of British dates, including two spectacular nights at Wembley, and by the time the sold-out tour drew to a close in Salisbury on 21 December, the album had topped the UK chart.

Troubles on tour

Opposite and above: John Bonham pictured in some rare moments of relaxation in 1971. The hot-rod Model T Ford had been bought in Boston the previous autumn.

The band left England in February 1972 for their one and only tour of Australia and New Zealand. The tour would prove a success, but got off to a bad start when they were refused entry to Singapore where they had been due to perform a warm-up show, while their first night in Perth was marred by crowd trouble and a drugs raid back at the hotel. After the tour, Page and Plant headed to India, where this time they would get the chance to record with local musicians, but back in England in April, Plant barely had time to celebrate the birth of his son Karac, as the band returned to recording, this time at Mick Jagger's country estate, Stargroves. After a couple of European warm-ups, it was back to America for a June tour, and thanks to the no-nonsense negotiating style of Peter Grant, they would now be receiving an unprecedented 90 per cent of gate receipts.

Los Angeles 1972

Above: Led Zeppelin inside Rodney's English Disco in LA with various groupies, including Sable Starr and Lori Maddox. Led Zeppelin's eighth North American tour opened at Detroit's Cobo Hall on 6 June, and would conclude at the Tucson Community Centre, Arizona, at the end of the month. Most of the shows were sold out and Zeppelin were at times performing for over two and a half hours, enabling them to preview material such as "Over The Hills And Far Away", "The Crunge" and "Dancing Days" from their as yet unreleased fifth album. However, the tour was somewhat overshadowed by that of the Rolling Stones, who were simultaneously traversing the US in support of their recently released *Exile On Main Street* LP. Towards the end of the June, Led Zeppelin performed at the LA forum and the Long Beach Arena in California, following which they would indulge themselves at their hotel of choice, the Continental Hyatt House, or the "Riot House" as it had become known, and clubs such as Rodney Bingenheimer's English Disco, where Jimmy Page was to meet Lori Maddox.

Opposite: Page in a limo outside Rodney's English Disco.

Cliques and Clubs

Opposite and above: Page and Bonham with Lori Maddox, Los Angeles, June 1972. Los Angeles had become one of Led Zeppelin's favourite US cities, not least because of the nightlife associated with such clubs as Rodney's English Disco, and the Rainbow Bar and Grill. The groupies that frequented these haunts were undoubtedly a particular attraction, and since their first jaunt to the states in late 1968 and early 1969, Zeppelin had commanded the attention of cliques such as the GTOs and the Plaster Casters. However, in 1972, they began to hang out with a new generation of groupies that included Sable Starr and Lori Maddox. Meeting Maddox in June, Jimmy Page rapidly found himself besotted, despite the fact that he was then romantically linked with Pamela Des Barres of the GTOs, and was in a long-term relationship with French model Charlotte Martin, who had recently borne him a daughter, Scarlet.

Biggest UK tour

Opposite and above: Led Zeppelin in Cardiff. When the US tour came to an end, Zeppelin spent some time at Electric Lady Studios in New York, before returning to England where they would get the chance to enjoy a three month break from any touring or recording commitments – although Page would busy himself putting finishing touches to the fifth album in the studio of his recently acquired home, Plumpton Place in Sussex. By October the band was ready to hit the road once more, and so they headed east, for a second tour of Japan, where "The Song Remains The Same" and "The Rain Song" would receive their live premières. According to Richard Cole, the band would also receive their introduction to heroin during the tour, which he had mistakenly purchased in the belief that he was buying cocaine. Returning to Britain, Led Zeppelin announced plans for their biggest UK tour yet, and when tickets went on sale in early November, they sold out within a matter of hours. The first leg of the tour began at the very end of the month in Newcastle, taking in such cities as Glasgow, Manchester, Cardiff and Brighton, before closing with two shows at London's Alexandra Palace just before Christmas.

Houses of the Holy

Opposite and above: The year 1973 had barely begun when Zeppelin resumed their UK tour in Sheffield. Unfortunately Plant was suffering with flu on the opening night, having hitch-hiked to the venue in bad weather when his car broke down. As the tour progressed, Plant's voice improved, and the fans responded well to both new material such as "Dancing Days" and "The Ocean", and old favourites such as "Dazed and Confused", which included Page's bowing technique. In Aberystwyth however, the band were in for something of a shock when they found themselves performing before a particularly reserved audience, which seemed largely to consist of local dignitaries. Better shows followed in Bradford, Southampton and Scotland, before the tour finally came to a close in Preston at the end of January. By this time, the release of Led Zeppelin's fifth album *Houses of the Holy* was already overdue, but it would be further delayed by issues with the sleeve art, which was now becoming a perennial problem for the band.

Houses of Holy

Left: The band pictured in June 1973. Finally released in late March, by April *Houses of the Holy* had topped the UK album chart, and it was poised to do the same in the US just as Led Zeppelin embarked upon the first leg of their mammoth ninth North American tour. The tour opened at the Atlanta Stadium in May and Led Zeppelin set an attendance record, attracting a crowd of around 49,200. The following day it was on to Tampa and another landmark performance – shattering the Beatles' record attendance figure of over 55,000, which had been set at Shea Stadium in 1965.

Above: Kezar Stadium, San Francisco. Towards the end of the month, Jimmy Page injured a finger in San Diego, leading to the postponement of one performance in LA. On 2 June the boys were back in the saddle, headlining an all day festival at Kezar Stadium which also featured Roy Harper, The Tubes, and Lee Michaels.

Bonham "The Beast"

Above: Of all Led Zeppelin's members, John Bonham had developed the biggest reputation for causing mayhem, and since his arrest in France earlier in the year for trashing a hotel room, he had been nicknamed "La Bête", or "The Beast". On his 25th birthday, two days before the Kezar Stadium show, he had let off some steam by throwing George Harrison into a swimming pool. Backstage at Kezar, promoter Bill Graham was in for some similar treatment. With tensions running high due to a late start, Bonham decided to cool Graham off with a bucket of water before the band returned to the stage for their encore. Since the mid-1960s impresario Bill Graham had carved out a successful career as a manager as well as a promoter, and was more used to being treated like rock royalty, rather than the victim of a prank. However, he would make a substantial sum from the concert, which reportedly earned Led Zeppelin around $320,000.
Opposite: The following day the band took to the stage of the LA Forum.

Coming "home" to LA

Above and opposite: Jones and Bonham on stage at the LA Forum, 3 June 1973. Back in their spiritual home, Led Zeppelin concluded the first part of their tour with an exceptional performance, which featured a half hour rendition of "Dazed and Confused" and a 20 minute "Whole Lotta Love" medley, which included Freddie King's "I'm Going Down" and Bo Diddley's "I'm a Man", a song that had provided the Yardbirds with a *Billboard* top twenty hit in 1965. The show drew to a close with an organ solo from Jones, which acted as the introduction to Plant's "Thank You". Prior to leaving England, Led Zeppelin had spent a great deal of time in rehearsals, largely working on a stage show and new arrangements that would incorporate Jones' increasing use of the electric piano and Mellotron, and to test out a more sophisticated lighting rig than they had previously employed. The tour was also marked by a thawing in the relationship between the band and the press, which was no doubt improved by the employment of PR man Danny Goldberg.

Taking a break

Opposite and above: On stage at the LA Forum in June. With a month's break before their tour of North America resumed, Zeppelin enjoyed a holiday in Hawaii before returning to the UK. Already the owner of Jennings Farm near Kidderminster, Robert Plant was to buy a working sheep farm on the Welsh coast while Jimmy Page added to his property portfolio by outbidding David Bowie for Richard Harris' Tower House in West London – an imposing gothic building that had been designed and decorated by the Victorian artist and architect William Burgess. Soon afterwards Page also opened an occult bookshop and publishing house called The Equinox Booksellers and Publishers in nearby Kensington High Street, reflecting his interest in all things mystical. However, it was his fascination with the works of the hedonistic occultist Alistair Crowley that most attracted the attention of the press and public.

Commuting on The Starship

Opposite and above: By the time Led Zeppelin arrived in Chicago for the second leg of their American tour in July, Richard Cole had chartered *The Starship* – a private jet that would allow them to hole up in their hotel of choice in New York or LA and commute to surrounding cities. They had hired jets before, but *The Starship* was different; this was a converted Boeing 720B – a 40-seat luxury liner with room for Led Zeppelin and their entourage, housing a club room, bedroom, shower, and a lounge bar complete with an organ. But despite such creature comforts, as the tour chugged relentlessly on from one three hour show to the next, Zeppelin were beginning to show signs of fatigue. Page was still suffering with his injured hand, Plant's voice lacked consistency, and the band were becoming jumpy when firecrackers were set off at their shows – no doubt as a result of the mounting number of death threats being received. On 18 July in Vancouver, the situation worsened when something Plant consumed backstage was apparently spiked and the show had to be brought to an abrupt end.

Climax of the 1973 tour

Opposite and right: Page and Plant at Madison Square Garden, July 1973. Prior to the tour, the film maker Joe Massot had approached Peter Grant about making a Led Zeppelin movie, but his offer had been turned down. As the 1973 tour neared its finale, however, Grant decided to fly in Massot and his crew from England to capture the last of the shows. Filming began in Baltimore and Pittsburgh on 23 and 24 July, but the real focus of attention were the three consecutive nights at Madison Square Garden that brought the tour to its conclusion, and which would ultimately form the basis of the film *The Song Remains The Same*. On the last night, 29 July, Zeppelin gave an explosive performance, but just as the entire tour had been characterised by massive highs and lows, there would be a final unfortunate twist, when $203,000 was stolen from the band's safe deposit box at their New York hotel. Back in England, Page, Plant, Bonham and Jones dispersed to their homes, where Massot recorded some individual film sequences. In November they regrouped at Headley Grange, but meanwhile Jones set about producing an album for Madeline Bell, while Page resumed work on a soundtrack for the cult director and fellow Crowley enthusiast Kenneth Anger.

Swan Song

Above: Robert Plant with fans in LA in 1973. During the summer of 1973, Led Zeppelin had reached peaks of both inspiration and decadence, working and partying perhaps harder than ever before. But as 1974 began to unfold, an opportunity arose that would provide the band and others with a new creative outlet. Their contract with Atlantic Records having expired, in January Led Zeppelin announced that they would be founding their own record label.

Opposite: Plant at the "Riot House" with Bad Company's Boz Burrell and Simon Kirke, May 1974. Having spent the first few months of the year writing and recording at Headley Grange, by May Led Zeppelin and Peter Grant were ready to launch their Swan Song label, which would issue records by such artists as Maggie Bell, and the Pretty Things, as well as Led Zeppelin themselves. The first release was to be the eponymous debut album of new British supergroup Bad Company, who accompanied Zeppelin to the lavish parties held in New York and Los Angeles to celebrate Swan Song's formation.

The Song Remains the Same

Opposite: Plant in LA. Led Zeppelin maintained a relatively low profile at the Swan Song launch parties, as they would throughout 1974 as they enjoyed a break from touring, but behind the scenes the new album was taking shape, as was *The Song Remains The Same* film project. Disappointed by Joe Massot's slow progress, by late summer he had been replaced as director by Peter Clifton, with the result that the band assembled at Shepperton Film Studios in August to shoot additional material for the live sequences.

Right: Page during a performance with Roy Harper. Although Led Zeppelin would not perform live as a band in 1974, each of them took to the stage at different times during the year, either alone or in various combinations. In February, Page, Plant and Bonham joined Roy Harper at London's Rainbow Theatre, whilst Jones made an appearance with Harper and Pink Floyd's Dave Gilmour in Hyde Park in August. Towards the end of the year, Page appeared at several shows with new label-mates Bad Company, whose debut LP had by now hit the top of the US charts.

Part Three

The Song Remains The Same

Physical Graffiti

Above: Page on stage in Chicago, 20 January 1975. As 1975 began, it had been almost a year and a half since Led Zeppelin's last performance at Madison Square Garden, but with their new double album *Physical Graffiti* about to hit the record shops, the Zeppelin behemoth prepared to take America by storm once more. After two warm up shows in Rotterdam and Brussels, which showcased the new songs "Sick Again", "Trampled Underfoot", "The Wanton Song", "In My Time of Dying" and the majestic, eastern-influenced opus, "Kashmir", Led Zeppelin crossed the Atlantic to kick-start their tenth North American tour in Minneapolis on 18 January. Once again Jimmy Page was nursing a badly injured finger, this time having caught his hand in a train door in London, and two days into the tour in Chicago Robert Plant came down with the flu, which would adversely affect his vocals for much of the tour.

Opposite: Robert Plant on stage in Indianapolis, 25 January 1975.

Dazed and Confused

Above: John Bonham in his "Clockwork Orange" outfit at Madison Square Garden, New York, February 1975. With Jimmy's finger beginning to recover, "Dazed and Confused" was returned to the set for the first time at Madison Square Garden. In fact, it was the first time that Led Zeppelin had performed the song live since 29 July 1973, at the very same venue. The avant-garde writer William S. Burroughs attended the show, following which he and Page conducted a two-way interview for *Crawdaddy!* magazine.

Opposite: The following night, Led Zeppelin were due to perform at the Boston Garden, however, the show was replaced by an extra date at the Nassau Coliseum, Uniondale, after hundreds of fans waiting to buy tickets in Boston ransacked the venue, causing an estimated $75,000 worth of damage. The band played two further shows at Nassau later in the month, with the Faces' Ronnie Wood joining the band for an encore on the 13th. Soon afterwards, Zeppelin closed the first leg of the tour in St Louis, following which Page and Plant headed to Dominica for a holiday.

Record rise to the top

Opposite and right: Led Zeppelin on stage at the LA Forum, March 1975. By the time the second leg of the tour began in Houston, Texas, on 27 February, Led Zeppelin's sixth album, *Physical Graffiti*, had been released. It was their first to be issued on Swan Song, and was an instant success. Having turned platinum on advance orders alone, the album entered the US chart at number three – an unprecedented feat at the time – and reached the top in record time. As usual the album also rocketed to number one in the UK. Despite Page's injury, Plant's fragile voice, and the fact that Bonham was now suffering from a stomach complaint, the tour was also proving to be a massive success. Once again the band was jetting around on the *Starship*, while onstage they were utilizing an even more impressive sound and lighting system, which included smoke machines, projectors and lasers. The tour closed with three shows at the LA Forum, the last of which, on 27 March, ran for almost three and a half hours and included a 46-minute rendition of "Dazed and Confused". Two days later Led Zeppelin scored another major coup in the US, with all six of their albums simultaneously charting on the *Billboard* Top 200.

US press won round

Opposite: Plant and Phil May of the Pretty Things being interviewed by the radio DJ and television personality J.J. Jackson on NBC's *Midnight Special*. Led Zeppelin had signed the Pretty Things to their Swan Song record label in 1974, holding a lavish Halloween party at Chislehurst Caves in Kent to celebrate the release of their *Silk Torpedo* LP. Similarly when their second album, *Savage Eye*, was issued in the US in 1975, a party was held at the Shrine in Los Angeles, where John Bonham reportedly had to be prevented from attacking the British music journalist Andy McConnell. At this time, Plant began to be more comfortable talking to the American media and in turn the US press now seemed to accept that led Zeppelin had earned their status as the biggest band in the world.

Right: Robert Plant on stage in the US, 1975.

Tax exiles

Opposite and above: London, 1975. Even before Led Zeppelin completed their North American tour, they had decided that the time was now right to take their dramatic new show to England, for what would be their first performances on home soil since January 1973. In mid-March three shows were announced, to be held at London's Earls Court in May. However, when all the tickets sold out within a matter of hours, two further nights had to be added to the itinerary. It was also around this time that Peter Grant and Led Zeppelin were advised that they would have to begin living as tax exiles if they were to avoid giving up much of the fortune that they had so far amassed in 1975, and so would have to leave the UK almost as soon as the Earls Court shows were over. None of the group's members were particularly enthralled with the idea, least of all John Bonham who particularly hated being away from his family, but financially there was little option. At the first of the Earls Court shows on 17 May, Robert Plant could not resist aiming some barbed comments in the direction of the British chancellor, Denis Healey.

Returning to London

Left: Robert Plant at Earls Court. Not only had it been over two years since Led Zeppelin had performed in the UK, but with the tax situation as it was, Peter Grant and the boys were acutely aware that the handful of dates at Earls Court might well be Led Zeppelin's last in Britain for some time to come. As a result, the shows were seen as an opportunity to thank the British fans for their support over the years, and while no expense was to be spared in terms of production, ticket prices were kept low.

High-tech live shows

Right: Jimmy Page plays at Earls Court. The high-tech sound and light system that Zeppelin had employed on their North American tour, which included a 70,000 watt speaker system, was flown over from the States, as were Texas-based Showco's own crew to oversee the installation and smooth running of all the equipment at the venue. In addition, a huge video screen was erected above the stage that would show close ups of the band as they played – one of the first times such technology had been employed in this way at a rock concert.

Musical prowess

Opposite and left: For five nights between 17 and 25 May, Led Zeppelin played what have come to be regarded as some of the best shows of their entire career, at what was then Britain's largest indoor arena. The shows were introduced by some of British radio's biggest rock DJs, including Jonnie Walker, David "Kid" Jensen, Nicky Horne, Bob Harris and Alan Freeman, and each night saw Led Zeppelin in fine form as they provided their audiences with what was essentially a three hour retrospective, covering material from each of their six albums – from "Dazed and Confused", which saw Jimmy Page illuminated by a pyramid of lasers as he dragged the violin bow across his guitar strings, to "Kashmir", a song that Led Zeppelin not only regarded as one of their greatest achievements, but which had also served to convince a number of dissenting critics of Zeppelin's musical prowess. In fact by the end of the last show, which ran close to four hours in length, Led Zeppelin had not only wowed some 85,000 fans, but had also finally won over the more traditionally conservative sections of the British press.

Plant injured

Opposite: Plant on stage. Still riding high on the buzz of the Earls Court shows, Led Zeppelin left the UK for Montreux, where plans were drawn up for a world tour. Before the tour there was time for a break and Robert and Maureen Plant travelled to Morocco, where they would be joined by Jimmy Page, before heading to Rhodes, accompanied by Jimmy's girlfriend Charlotte and daughter Scarlet. However, on 4 August disaster struck when the Plants' rental car left the road and collided with a tree, seriously injuring Page and his wife. Richard Cole chartered a plane to fly them back to Britain for treatment, but while Maureen recovered in an English hospital, tax-exile Plant was forced to fly on to Jersey to recuperate.

Above: In September, with touring plans shelved, Page and Plant headed to Los Angeles to begin writing new material. Holed up in a Malibu beach house with Plant wheelchair-bound and miserable it was perhaps a miracle that anything was accomplished, but by the end of the year the band had recorded and mixed their seventh album *Presence*. Despite the year's misfortunes, the band also swept the board at the annual *Melody Maker* awards in London, with Plant and Bonham (pictured with Maggie Bell) on hand to collect an unprecedented seven first-place awards.

WILSHIRE
LED ZEPPELIN
THE SONG REMAINS THE SAME
WILSHIRE
LED ZEPPELIN
THE SONG REMAINS THE SAME

The Song Remains the Same

Opposite and above: Determined to keep the Zeppelin aloft, Jimmy Page had largely taken control of the sessions for *Presence* and, although it would prove to be one of the band's lowest-selling LPs, massive advance orders would help send it to the top of the charts on both sides of the Atlantic in the spring of 1976. Meanwhile, with Plant still in recovery and the band off the road, Page turned his attention to producing the soundtrack album that would accompany the opening of Led Zeppelin's movie *The Song Remains the Same*. By now the film had been some three years in the making and had suffered from a host of production problems, including having had two directors and numerous setbacks with the filming of performance footage. The band members and Peter Grant also had some misgivings about the fantasy sequences that they had shot, but on 20 October, 1976, the film received its world première in New York, accompanied by a quadraphonic sound system courtesy of Showco, and attended by a host of celebrity guests, including Led Zeppelin themselves.

Box-office draw

Opposite and above: Two days later *The Song Remains the Same* opened in several other US cities, including LA, where Led Zeppelin were once again in attendance, as they would be for the movie's European première in London on 4 November. *Melody Maker*'s Chris Charlesworth supplied a positive review, which was something of a surprise considering that he had been set upon by Richard Cole in New York, but in general the critics did little to disguise their contempt for the film, and it was widely derided for its apparent self indulgence. Nevertheless *The Song Remains the Same* proved to be quite a big draw at the box-office, at least initially, while the double soundtrack LP was more predictably and convincingly successful, hitting the UK number one spot a little more than a week after its release and stalling at number two in the US, where it was held from the top by Stevie Wonder's highly acclaimed double album *Songs in the Key of Life*.

Changing musical landscape

Opposite and above: In late 1976 and early 1977, Led Zeppelin began to prepare for a return to touring, going into the studio in London to work on live arrangements for songs such as "Nobody's Fault But Mine" and the multi-layered "Achilles Last Stand" from the *Presence* LP. By this time, with the punk phenomenon starting to gather momentum, the musical landscape was beginning to change dramatically on both sides of the Atlantic, and although some of these new groups were openly hostile to Led Zeppelin – regarding them as rock and roll dinosaurs, Page, Plant and Bonham took the time to check out bands such as the Damned at the Roxy in London. In Los Angeles Led Zeppelin received a warmer welcome at an album launch party for the all-girl, punk rock outfit the Runaways, no doubt because of their long-standing relationship with the Runaways self-styled Svengali and sometime singer Kim Fowley (above), with whom Jimmy Page and John Paul Jones had recorded in the mid-1960s.

the
Runaways
JOAN JETT

Chicago 1977

Left: Bonham in a publicity still for *The Song Remains the Same*. In early February 1977, Zeppelin announced plans for a world tour, to launch in the US before the end of the month. However, the start date had to be postponed to the beginning of April, as Robert Plant was suffering from laryngitis and his leg was still not fully healed. Also the use of heroin had become prevalent amongst various members of the Led Zeppelin entourage, manager Peter Grant had recently split from his wife, and there was no new material to mark the group's long-awaited comeback. Nevertheless, tickets for the entire tour sold out in days, and US audiences welcomed the return of the sit-down acoustic set – as did Plant, whose leg was causing considerable pain. On 9 April Led Zeppelin took to the stage at the Chicago Stadium but after barely an hour the show had to be cancelled as Page staggered off stage suffering from stomach cramps.

Record breaking in Michigan

Right: Led Zeppelin on stage in Cleveland, Ohio, 27 April, 1977. With Jimmy's stomach settled and Plant's initial trepidation subsided, Led Zeppelin rapidly found their form during the first leg of what was to be the biggest and most financially successful tour of their career. However, several of the early dates were blighted by events beyond the band's control, ranging from problems with the sound system to crowd trouble. On 13 April more than 20 people were arrested in Saint Paul, Minnesota as they tried to gatecrash the concert, while less than a week later, an estimated 1000 fans attempted to storm the Riverfront Coliseum, Cincinnati. Worse still, a young fan was mortally injured at the second Cincinnati show after falling from an upper level of the stadium. The first leg of the tour concluded on 30 April at the Pontiac Silverdome, Michigan, in front of a record-breaking audience of 76,229 – just topping the record set by The Who at the same venue in 1975. Led Zeppelin gave a solid performance, but John Paul Jones would later complain that you could barely see or hear the audience from the stage.

Ivor Novello award

Opposite: Robert Plant and John Paul Jones at the Grosvenor Hotel, London. With a little over two weeks until their eleventh North American tour resumed in Birmingham, Alabama, Plant, Bonham and Jones returned to Britain, while Page headed for Cairo. Long intrigued by the city that had also entranced his hero Alistair Crowley, Page was finally convinced to make the trip after watching some newsreel footage that showed a zeppelin flying over the ancient pyramids. By 12 May, Page had returned, to join his bandmates and Peter Grant at the Grosvenor hotel, as they collected an Ivor Novello award for their Outstanding Contribution to British Music.

Above: Robert Plant playing football in a Los Angeles park during the 1977 tour. In May Led Zeppelin were back in the States preparing to embark upon the second leg of their tour. Plant's leg was holding up well, apparently as a result of having attended some training sessions with his beloved local football team, Wolverhampton Wanderers. An avid fan of the game, Plant had also been known to take part in matches against Bonham, with the two of them playing for rival pub teams in the Midlands.

Alabama and Louisiana

Opposite and above: Zeppelin on stage at Madison Square Garden, June 1977. The second leg of the tour got off to a very good start with performances in Alabama and Louisiana, but by the third show, in Texas, signs of the disorder that had marred some of the April shows were creeping back in. Several arrests were made after fans caused extensive damage in Houston, and on 3 June in Tampa, Florida, full scale rioting erupted when the show was cancelled due to torrential rain. More than 70 people had to be hospitalized, including several policemen, but Peter Grant was unrepentant and the promoters, Concerts West, were forced to accept responsibility for the debacle, having advertised the show as a "rain or shine" event. Four days later, Led Zeppelin arrived in New York, to begin a run of six shows at the Madison Square Garden.

Page struggling to cope

Above: Between 7 and 14 June, Led Zeppelin entertained some 120,000 people at New York's Madison Square Garden, where Robert Plant jokingly dedicated the opening show to the Queen of England, who was then celebrating her Silver Jubilee. The shows were certainly a highlight of the tour, with Zeppelin performing at the height of their abilities. For much of the tour Jimmy Page looked particularly striking, taking to the stage clad in his white silk "dragon suit", with his eyes often hidden behind dark glasses, but offstage both friends and associates, including the journalist Dave Schulps, noted with concern how thin and pale the guitarist was becoming. Tour manager Richard Cole attests that by this time both he and Page were beginning to succumb to the ravages of heroin addiction, although Page would maintain that he remained in control when it really counted.

Opposite: Plant on stage in Los Angeles.

Caesar's Chariot

Opposite and above: From New York, Led Zeppelin and their entourage flew on to California. They were no longer using the *Starship*, which had been grounded with engine trouble earlier in the year, but were still travelling in style, having hired *Caesar's Chariot*, a luxury airliner belonging to the Caesar's Palace Hotel in Las Vegas. On 19 June Led Zeppelin performed before a crowd of over 14,000 at the San Diego Sports Arena, and although there were no incidents of violence, several arrests were made outside the venue as the police cracked down on ticket touts and inebriated fans. Two days later, the band opened a run of six sold-out shows at the Los Angeles Forum, where they would set yet another record by playing to a total of 108,000 fans. Over the course of the six nights, the quality of Led Zeppelin's performances was slightly variable, with Page's playing being somewhat erratic on the second night, but the first of the shows was a stirring affair, with Page dropping into a Hendrix-like rendition of "The Star Spangled Banner" during his solo slot.

Los Angeles Forum

Right and opposite: On 23 June, on the third night of the Los Angeles Forum shows, the audience were treated to the surprise appearance of The Who's Keith Moon, who took to the stage to join John Bonham for his "Moby Dick" drum solo, before returning to play timpani during the encores of "Whole Lotta Love" and "Rock and Roll", and attempting to join Plant at the microphone for a rendition of Eddie Cochran's "C'mon Everybody", much to the amusement of all concerned. Offstage however, the behaviour of Bonham and Moon – who was equally well known for his hell-raising – was rather less entertaining. The following evening, with a night off from performing, the pair visited LA's Comedy Store, only to be ejected on account of Moon's drunken heckling. Meanwhile Bonham's own drinking, which had always been very heavy, seemed to many to have spiralled right out of control as he attempted to live up to his own mythology.

Electrifying performance

Opposite and above: On 27 June 1977, the second leg of the North American tour came to an end with the last of six shows at the Forum in Los Angeles. Around 8 pm the restless audience was subdued by an announcement from the stage, and then 20 minutes later, Led Zeppelin launched into an electrifying performance that incorporated some heavy jamming, numerous improvisations, and a startling use of effects, which extended to both Bonham's drums and Jones' piano during their solo sections. The set was also marked by some surprising inclusions, such as an acoustic rendition of Arthur Crudup's "That's Alright (Mama)" – made famous as Elvis Presley's first single – and a hard rockabilly version of Jerry Lee Lewis' "It'll Be Me", which closed the show as an encore, Plant having introduced it as a song that would be included on the next album. The show over, Led Zeppelin headed straight for the airport and back to Britain for a well-earned rest.

Tragic news for Robert Plant

Opposite and above: Led Zeppelin onstage at the Oakland Coliseum, July 1977. On 17 July 1977, Led Zeppelin resumed their epic tour of the States at the Seattle Kingdome, in front of a crowd of over 62,000 fans. This was followed three days later by a shambolic performance in Arizona, and then it was on to California for two consecutive appearances at the "Day on the Green" festival at the Oakland-Alameda County Coliseum. The occasion was meant to be a celebratory affair, but was marred when one of promoter Bill Graham's security staff was subjected to a savage beating by Peter Grant and his head of security John Bindon. Richard Cole and John Bonham were also involved in the incident, and two days later the four of them were arrested at their hotel on assault charges. Having been bailed, Bonham and Cole travelled with Plant to New Orleans, where Led Zeppelin were next due to perform, but arriving at their hotel, Robert Plant received an urgent call from his wife, and the terrible news that their son Karac had died suddenly from a respiratory virus.

Future in doubt

Right: Robert Plant at Knebworth with his daughter, Carmen. Distraught at the death of his son, Robert Plant immediately returned to England to be with his family, and the remaining US tour dates were cancelled. Meanwhile thoughtless press reports began to emerge, which focused on a Led Zeppelin curse, supposedly engendered by Jimmy's interest in the occult. Rumours of a split abounded, and indeed, for some time Led Zeppelin's entire future seemed to hang in the balance. In May 1978, the band took its first tentative steps towards a return – convening at Clearwell Castle in the Forest of Dean to rehearse – and by the end of the year, the recording of a new album had begun in Sweden, this time with John Paul Jones at the helm. The LP was completed in early 1979, and on 22 May Led Zeppelin announced their intention to headline a huge outdoor show at Knebworth Park, Hertfordshire.

Opposite: Peter Grant, Robert Plant and John Paul Jones, backstage at Knebworth, August 1979.

Knebworth

Opposite and above: Led Zeppelin onstage at Knebworth, August 1979. By early July, with rehearsals for Knebworth well under way, a second date was added due to ticket demand. Perhaps Led Zeppelin felt that in their absence British interest had waned, but thousands of fans were desperate for a chance to see them perform in Britain – the first time they had done so since Earls Court in 1975 – and over 200,000 tickets were sold in just two days. Following two warm-up shows in their old stomping ground of Copenhagen, where the new songs "Hot Dog" and "In The Evening" were to receive their live previews, Led Zeppelin made their triumphant return to the British stage at Knebworth on 4 and 11 August, to a rapturous reception. Reviews were somewhat mixed, and even members of Led Zeppelin would later criticise their own performance, but almost everyone seemed to agree that the atmosphere had been truly magical. Ticket sales and the official capacity of the venue aside, it was later suggested that attendance figures had been close to 200,000 for each night.

In Through the Out Door

A publicity shot for Knebworth 1979. Originally due for release prior to the Knebworth Festival, Led Zeppelin issued their eighth studio album, *In Through The Out Door* on 8 August, four days after the first of the Knebworth shows. In the UK the album entered the chart at number one, while in the US it would reach the top of the *Billboard* chart within a week, having entered the listings at number 10. The excitement produced by the band's return to performing, and the appearance of the new LP – which featured six marginally different sleeve designs but came clad in a brown paper bag – had the somewhat unexpected effect of sparking massive interest in Zeppelin's entire back catalogue, to the extent that by late October, all nine of their LPs could be found on the *Billboard* Top 200 in the same week.

John Bonham: death by misadventure

28 November 1979, Plant, Jones and Bonham receive an award at the Waldorf Hotel in London. As the new decade began Led Zeppelin's latest single, "Fool In The Rain", was hovering just outside the US top 20, although little was heard from the band themselves until May, when their "Tour Over Europe" was announced. Beginning on 17 June in Dortmund, Peter Grant hoped that this outing would serve as a prelude to yet another North American tour, and by early September the plans were in place for a three-week stint across Canada and the US. On 24 September Led Zeppelin met for rehearsals at Bray Studios, before retiring to Jimmy's new home in nearby Windsor, where after several large drinks, John Bonham was helped to bed around midnight. The following afternoon, John Paul Jones and Robert Plant's assistant Benji LeFevre went to check on the sleeping drummer, only to discover that he had died in his sleep. On 8 October, an inquest recorded a verdict of "death by misadventure" and two months later Swan Song issued a statement explaining that the band could no longer continue.

Marshall
Marshall
Marshall

Part Four

A Whole Lot of Love

Coda

Opposite: Jimmy Page in 1982. In the immediate aftermath of John Bonham's tragic and untimely death, while the press churned out rumours of reunions and stories about "the Zeppelin curse", Robert Plant, Jimmy Page and John Paul Jones each retreated into a private world of grief and pain. But in 1981 and 1982, they began to forge new pathways. The self-effacing Jones found solace in the tranquillity of rural Devon, where he established a recording studio and taught composition, Plant resurfaced on stage with the Honeydrippers, before going on to record the hit solo album *Pictures at Eleven*, and Page recorded the soundtrack to Michael Winner's movie *Death Wish II*. However, Jimmy Page also had some unfinished business to attend to, in the form of producing Led Zeppelin's final studio album, the aptly titled *Coda*, which was compiled from previously unreleased material.

Above: In 1983 Plant released another highly successful LP, *The Principle of Moments*, before embarking on his first solo tours of Britain and North America. Page meanwhile became involved with Ronnie Lane's multiple sclerosis charity ARMS, and in September performed at London's Royal Albert Hall alongside Eric Clapton (centre) and Jeff Beck (second from the right) – the first time that all three former Yardbirds guitarists had appeared on stage together.

Page and The Firm

Opposite and above: After the success of the London ARMS concert, a series of benefit shows were organised in the States, where Jimmy Page and Paul Rodgers, the singer-songwriter who had found fame with Free and Bad Company, began to discuss founding a new group. During the summer of 1984, Page made several live appearances alongside his old friend Roy Harper, with whom he was also collaborating on the album *Whatever Happened to Jugula?*, but by August, Page and Rodgers had set up The Firm, having been joined by bassist Tony Franklin and drummer Chris Slade. The band enjoyed successful tours of Britain, Europe and the US in 1985 and 1986, and also issued two albums, their eponymous debut in early 1985, followed by *Mean Business* a year later. The Firm would prove to be a rather short-lived project, disbanding soon after the release of the second album and the completion of a second US tour.

Led Zeppelin reunite for Live Aid

Opposite and above: Led Zeppelin at Live Aid, 13 July, 1985. Although John Bonham's death had perhaps hit Robert Plant the hardest – the two of them having been friends since the pre-Zeppelin days – by the mid-1980s Plant was enjoying considerable success, both with the Honeydrippers, with whom he recorded an EP of classic R&B material, and as a solo artist – his third album, *Shaken 'n' Stirred*, once again performing well on both sides of the Atlantic. He had also enjoyed successful tours of Britain, North America, Australasia and the Far East. While Page had contributed to the Honeydrippers EP, as well as a soundtrack album that Jones had recorded for another Michael Winner movie, the idea of a Led Zeppelin reunion must have seemed like a distant prospect indeed. However, in 1985, when numerous recording artists assembled to back Bob Geldof's drive to raise awareness of a terrible famine occurring in parts of Africa, Plant, Page and Jones would be among them.

Back on the world stage

Opposite and above: In early 1985, two star-studded charity singles emerged in response to Bob Geldof's anti-famine campaign – Band Aid's "Feed The World" and the USA for Africa's "We Are the World", neither of which featured any former Led Zeppelin members. However, when two Live Aid concerts were announced for the summer, to take place simultaneously in Britain and the US, Robert Plant signalled his desire to participate. Originally, the organizers proposed pairing Plant with Eric Clapton, but the singer was not keen. Instead he suggested performing at the concert with the Honeydrippers, with whom he would then be touring the States, but the magnitude of the event quickly convinced him that the time was right to reunite with Page and Jones. Both readily agreed, and on 13 July Led Zeppelin took to the stage in Philadelphia, with bassist Paul Martinez (enabling Jones to switch to keyboards during "Stairway to Heaven"), and drummers Phil Collins and Tony Thompson.

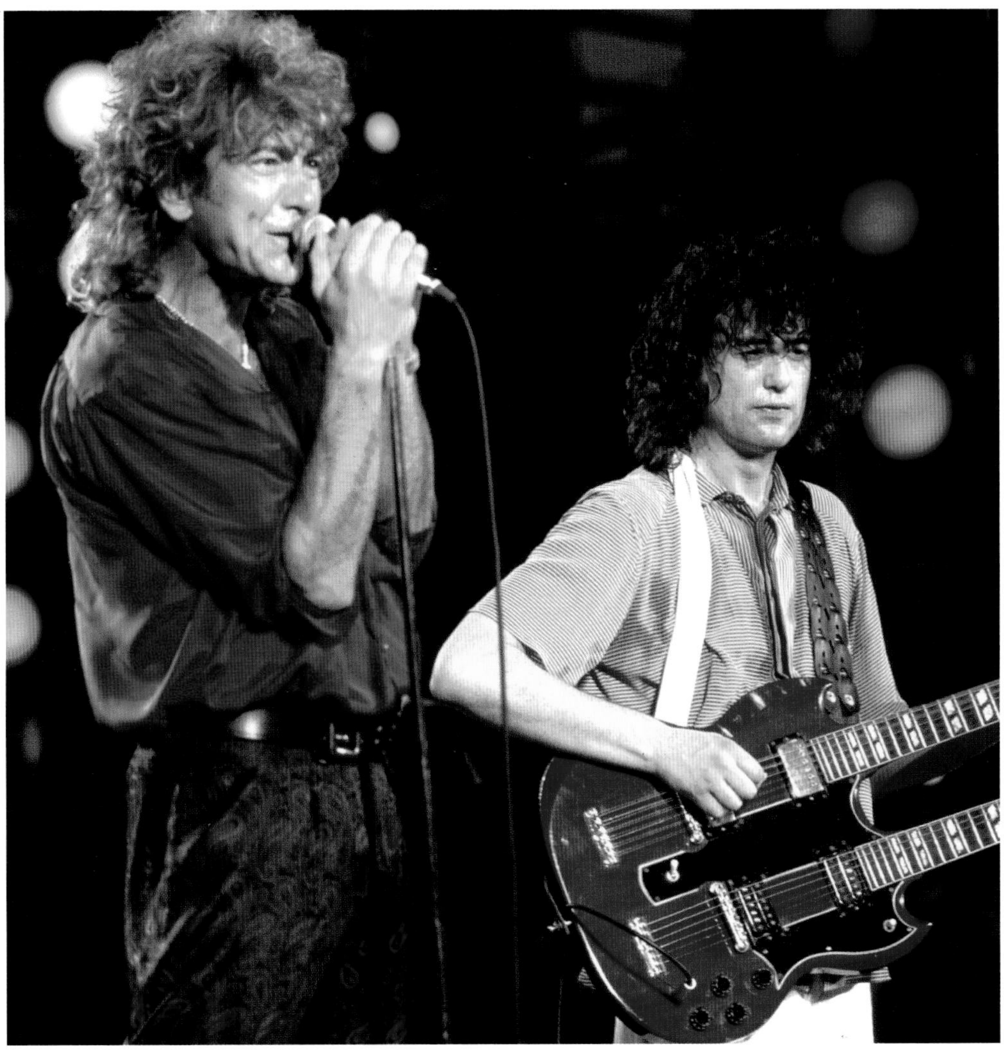

Self criticism in Philadelphia

Opposite and above: When Page, Plant and Jones took to the stage in Philadelphia, the crowd of over 100,000 erupted. It had been five years since the three musicians had all performed together, and for the fans and press alike the event ranked as one of the most awaited comebacks in the history of rock and roll. Page and Plant also appeared to revel in the occasion, although a combination of technical problems, Plant's sore throat and perhaps even a little nervousness, conspired to produce a somewhat lacklustre performance.

Looking back years later at their 20 minute set, which consisted of "Rock and Roll", "Whole Lotta Love" and "Stairway to Heaven", each of them expressed mixed emotions. They had all enjoyed sharing a stage once more, but Page and Plant were particularly critical of their actual performance, and when the Live Aid DVD came to be released in 2004, Led Zeppelin's set was notably absent, having been omitted at their own request.

Anniversary appearance

Opposite and above: Page and Plant on stage at Madison Square Garden, May, 1988. Spurred on by their appearance at Live Aid, in early 1986, Page, Plant and Jones reunited with drummer Tony Thompson for rehearsals near Bath, with a possible view to reforming Led Zeppelin. Within days, however, the venture was shelved, and each went their separate ways. Jones busied himself producing albums for the likes of Ben E. King and The Mission, Plant recorded his fourth album, *Now and Zen*, and Page began work on his first real solo venture, *Outrider*. Their paths would cross both in the studio and on the road in 1987, by which time Plant had begun to incorporate Zeppelin songs into his live sets, but the three of them would not play together again until 14 May 1988, when they agreed to reunite at Atlantic Records' 40th anniversary celebrations. Appearing at New York's Madison Square Garden, this time Led Zeppelin played with John Bonham's son Jason on drums, and performed a half-hour set consisting of "Kashmir", "Whole Lotta Love", "Misty Mountain Hop" and "Stairway to Heaven". There were moments of brilliance, particularly from Bonham, although Page and Plant had argued over the inclusion of "Stairway", and the mood was tense.

Plant's Magic Nirvana

Above: In addition to the Atlantic celebrations, Robert Plant attended the Nordoff-Robbins Music Therapy Foundation's Award and Auction dinner in New York in 1988, where he was to jam with Buckwheat Zydeco, Curt Smith and Neil Young. The surviving members of Led Zeppelin would give impromptu performances at Carmen Plant's 21st birthday in late 1989, and Jason Bonham's wedding in early 1990. Soon afterwards Plant released his fifth LP, *Magic Nirvana*, following which he spent the rest of the year undertaking an extensive tour.

Opposite: Jimmy Page and Jeff Beck (left) are pictured as the Yardbirds are inducted into the Rock and Roll Hall of Fame in 1992. Following *Outrider* Page focused on the band's back catalogue, resulting in the *Remasters* and *Led Zeppelin Boxed Set* albums of the early 1990s. Perhaps more surprisingly, he also began work on an album with David Coverdale, who Robert Plant liked to refer to as "David Cover-version", having previously singled him out as one of the main offenders amongst a new generation of Led Zeppelin imitators. The Coverdale-Page LP reached the top five on both sides of the Atlantic in 1993.

John Paul Jones

Opposite: As the 1990s began John Paul Jones was maintaining a decidedly low profile, although he was also being characteristically productive. He established a new studio near Bath and contributed to Peter Gabriel's *Us* album, assisted Page in track selection for the Zeppelin boxed sets, worked on music for Spanish theatre company La Sura Dels Baus, and acted as the musical director for the Seville Expo '92. In 1992 he also provided the orchestral arrangements for REM's hugely successful *Automatic for the People*, as well as producing the Butthole Surfers' *Independent Worm Saloon*. The following year he appeared live at the MTV Video Music Awards in California, where he performed "Are You Gonna Go My Way" with Lenny Kravitz, and in late 1994 he made a return to touring, spending almost two months on the road in Europe and North America with drummer Pete Thomas and the avant-garde performance artist and musician Diamanda Galas.

Right: In January 1995, Jones was on hand to collect Led Zeppelin's trophy for best International Artist at the American Music Awards.

Plant back on the road

Left: Plant on stage in Chicago, April 1995.

Opposite: Page, Plant and Jones with Jason and Zoe Bonham at the Waldorf-Astoria Hotel, 1995. In 1993, while Jimmy Page was pursuing a Led Zeppelin reunion, Plant headed back out on the road, this time in support of his latest album, *Fate of Nations*. In early '94, however, the two of them were reunited at the Alexis Korner Memorial Concert in Buxton, and by the summer they had accepted an invitation from MTV to record a performance for their *Unplugged* series. However, Plant's apparent desire to keep the Zeppelin spectre at arms length ensured that Jones would not be asked to participate, whilst his desire for artistic control would see the usual *Unplugged* studio format augmented with performances filmed in Wales and with local musicians in Morocco. Featuring a combination of reworked Zeppelin tunes and some new compositions, the 90-minute show was broadcast on 12 October, and two days later, *No Quarter: Jimmy Page and Robert Plant Unledded* was issued as an LP. In January 1995, Led Zeppelin were inducted into the Rock and Roll Hall of Fame at the Waldorf-Astoria Hotel in New York, where they performed with Jason Bonham and Aerosmith's Steven Tyler and Joe Perry, and soon afterwards, Page and Plant embarked upon a world tour.

Glastonbury

Opposite: Page and Plant on stage at the Glastonbury Festival, 25 June 1995.
Above: Page and Plant at the Shoreline Amphitheatre, Mountain View, California, 7 October 1995. Page and Plant spent much of 1995 on tour, traversing North America from the end of February until the end of May, before heading to Britain and Europe during the summer. On 25 June Page and Plant performed at the Glastonbury Festival in Somerset, and a month later, Peter Grant made his last public appearance at one of their Wembley Arena shows. He had long since fought his way free of the darkness that had engulfed him in the wake of Zeppelin's demise, but in late November, he would succumb to a fatal heart attack. Having completed another series of autumn dates in the US, Plant and Page returned to England to attend Grant's funeral with John Paul Jones. Long-time friend and former Swan Song VP Alan Callan read the eulogy and other guests included Jeff Beck, Chris Dreja, Phil May, Boz Burrell and Denny Laine.

A second album

Above: Page and Plant performing in Europe, 1998. In early 1996, Page and Plant continued their world tour with dates in South America, Japan and Australia, before taking a break to record their second album. Meanwhile, an edited of version of "Whole Lotta Love" became Led Zeppelin's first UK single release in 1997, peaking at number 21. Page and Plant's *Walking into Clarksdale* LP followed in early 1998, and they supported its release with an extensive tour of North America and Europe.

Opposite: The album yielded a Grammy Award-winning single in the form of "Most High", but that summer it was Page's somewhat incongruous collaboration with Puff Daddy that would propel him to the upper reaches of both the UK and US charts. Taken from the soundtrack to the *Godzilla* movie, Puff Daddy's "Come With Me", which sampled Led Zeppelin's "Kashmir" and featured extra guitar parts from Page, reached number 2 in Britain and number 4 on the *Billboard* Hot 100.

PLANET HOLLYWOOD

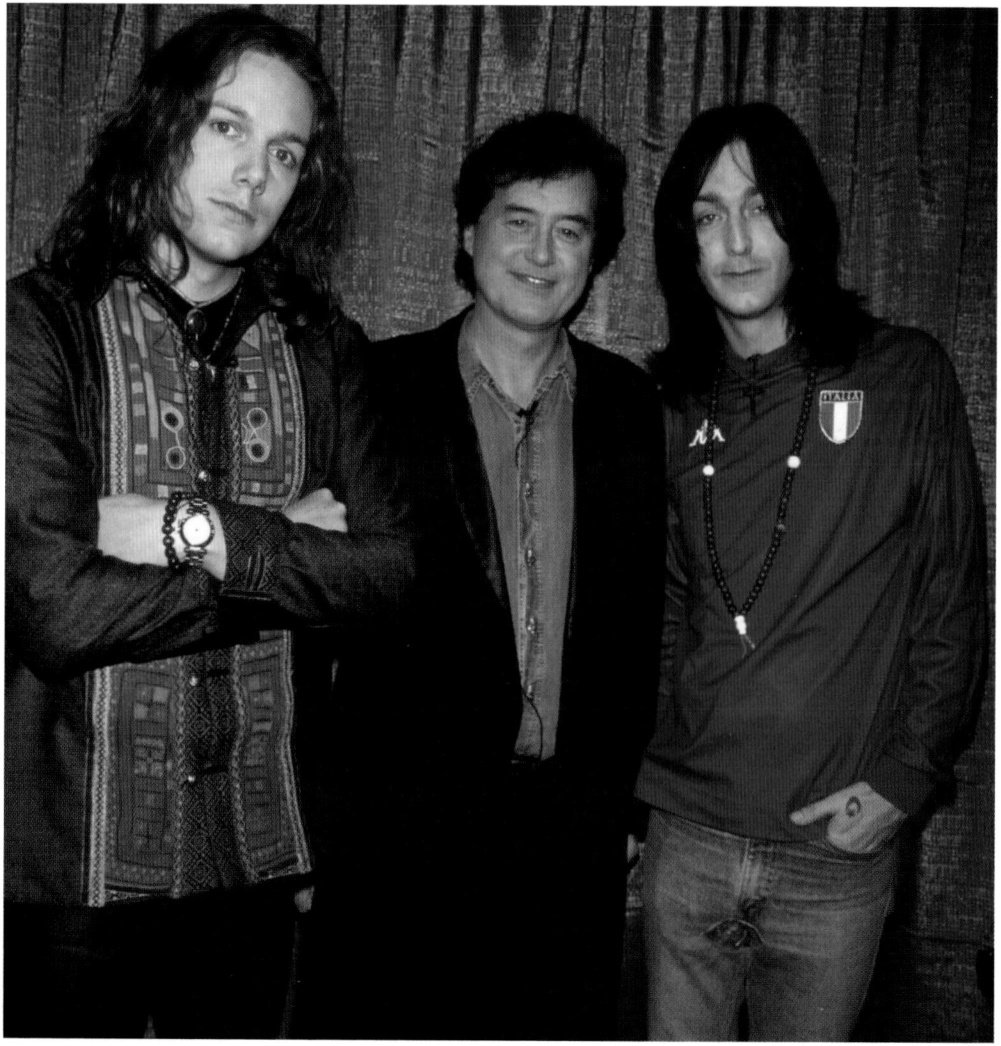

Plant and Page part again

Above: Jimmy Page on stage with the Black Crowes in LA, October 1999.

Opposite: Page with brothers Chris and Rich Robinson of the Black Crowes, at the release of their live album. In the spring of '99, having been awarded the Grammy for Best Hard Rock Performance, Page and Plant were supposedly due to continue their world tour in Australia, but as the months passed, it became clear that they had parted ways once more. Plant spent the rest of the year performing a series of low-key gigs around Britain with the Priory of Brion, a band that featured guitarist Kevyn Gammond, with whom he had performed in the Band of Joy. Page meanwhile teamed up with Southern US rockers the Black Crowes for a series of performances that would result in the release of the album *Live At The Greek* in early 2000. Page and the Crowes had planned a major tour for 2000, but this had to be scrapped after Page injured his back during a performance in the US in August.

Solo work

Opposite: John Paul Jones with the custom triple-necked instrument that had enabled him to recreate the overdubbed guitar parts on songs such as "Ten Years Gone" during Led Zeppelin's 1977 tour of the States. Jones had begun work on solo material at his new London studio in 1996, although his first album, *Zooma* did not emerge until late 1999. He supported its release with a North American tour in 2000, and the following year, having released his second LP, *The Thunderthief*, he returned to the States with the John Paul Jones Orchestra, opening shows for a re-formed King Crimson.

Above: Robert Plant at the Cheese and Grain, Frome, Somerset. In 1999, Plant and the Priory of Brion had begun by playing almost anonymously in pubs and small clubs in England and Wales, but throughout 2000, Plant took the band all over Britain and Europe, playing larger venues, and enjoying summer performances at a number of festivals, including Glastonbury, the Pistoia Blues Festival in Italy, the Nice Jazz Festival and the Cambridge Folk Festival. Having kicked off in Stoke-on-Trent in February, the tour finally concluded in Wolverhampton on 21 December.

DVS

Strange Sensation

Above: Robert Plant at Cadillac's 100th anniversary celebrations, August 2002. In 2001, Plant played a series of dates with his newly assembled band, the Strange Sensation, followed by an extensive tour of Britain, Europe and North America, and the release of the album, *Dreamland* in 2002. That same year, Led Zeppelin also licensed the commercial use of its music for the first time, allowing car manufacturer Cadillac to employ "Rock and Roll" as the soundtrack to its "Breakthrough" campaign. Plant appeared as guest of honour at their centennial celebrations in Detroit.

Opposite: Jimmy Page with Limp Bizkit's Fred Durst and Puddle of Mudd's Wes Scantlin at the MTV Europe Awards in Frankfurt, Germany. Having largely retreated from public view after a back injury, Page made a surprise guest appearance at the MTV Europe Awards in November 2001, joining "nu metal" artists Fred Durst and Wes Scantlin for a rendition of Led Zeppelin's "Thank You".

Biggest-selling music DVD

Opposite and left: While Robert Plant continued touring into 2003, Jimmy Page had once again been quietly working away in the studio, revisiting and re-mastering Led Zeppelin's vast archive of recorded material. His recent endeavours had already resulted in two "Best Of" compilation albums, but 2003 would see the release of the massively successful triple album *How the West Was Won*, gleaned from two performances in California in 1972, and the career-spanning *Led Zeppelin* DVD, which rapidly became the biggest-selling music DVD in history. That same year, Plant released the compilation album *Sixty Six to Timbuktu*, which covered his solo efforts from 1966 to 2003. While he seemed comfortable revisiting his own early works, he was clearly less keen to trade on Led Zeppelin's former glories, and a suggested reunion tour failed to materialise. The following year, John Paul Jones was probably the most highly visible of Zeppelin's former members when he embarked on a summer tour of the US with the Mutual Admiration Society, although Page would steal some of the limelight with his inauguration of the London Walk of Fame in August (left).

Lifetime Achievement Award

Above: Page and Ahmet Ertegun in Los Angeles, 2005.
On 13 February 2005, Led Zeppelin were honoured with a Lifetime Achievement Award at the 47th Annual Grammy Awards in Los Angeles. Both Jimmy Page and John Paul Jones were on hand to collect the award, while Atlantic Records "Founding Chairman", Ahmet Ertegun, was also in attendance. Along with Jerry Wexler, Ertegun had been central to the decision to sign Led Zeppelin to Atlantic in 1968, and he had remained a close friend to the group throughout their career. Later in the year he would receive the President's Merit Award from the National Academy of Recording Arts and Sciences, while Page was presented with an OBE at Buckingham Palace, and was made an honourary citizen of Rio de Janeiro in recognition of his charity work with the ABC Trust and Task Brazil. Meanwhile in February 2005, Robert Plant performed at two benefit concerts in Bristol, held in aid of victims of 2004's devastating Indian Ocean tsunami.
Opposite: Jimmy Page with John Paul Jones.

Mandela concert performance

Opposite and left: In early 2005, Robert Plant released *Mighty Rearranger*, his second album to feature backing from the Strange Sensation. As with their previous album, the LP would go on to earn two Grammy nominations, and was supported by an extensive tour of the UK, Europe and North America. Having completed two legs of the tour in March and April, on 11 June Plant and his band, which now included stalwarts of the Bristol trip-hop scene Clive Deamer and John Baggott, performed at Nelson Mandela's "46664 Arctic" concert in Tromso, Norway. The fourth in a series of concerts held in honour of Nelson Mandela and raising funds for his AIDS foundation, the event also featured Peter Gabriel, Annie Lennox, Bryan May, Sharon Corr, and Razorlight, as well as a host of other European and African musicians. Plant's set consisted of "Shine it all Around" and "The Enchanter" from his new album, as well as the Led Zeppelin classics "No Quarter", "When The Levee Breaks" and "Whole Lotta Love".

46664
ARCTIC
46664
ARCTIC

Plant at Chelmsford

Opposite and above: Robert Plant at the V Festival, Chelmsford, August 2005. Plant and the Strange Sensation continued their tour during the summer months, heading to North America for the remainder of June and much of July, before returning to Europe for the festival season – headlining slots at WOMAD in Reading and at Virgin's V Festival, which was held at two locations over two days in August. When Led Zeppelin had first disbanded, Plant had struggled with the idea of performing their material, but by now his sets typically included "No Quarter", "Black Dog", "Four Sticks", "Gallows Pole", "When The Levee Breaks" and "Whole Lotta Love". Rather than attempt faithful renditions of these songs, Plant and his band reinterpreted them – emphasizing the Moroccan and Eastern influences that had always infused Led Zeppelin's sound, and combining these with elements of trip-hop as well as blues-rock – not only reflecting Plant's longstanding fascination with non-Western music, but also his desire to remain artistically relevant.

Icon Award for Page

Opposite: Jimmy Page and Noel Gallagher of Oasis, at the *Q* Awards, October 2005. By 2005 Page appeared to be semi-retired from the music business and was devoting much of his time to raising his young children – something that had perhaps not always been easy during the heady days of Led Zeppelin, when the band were frequently on the road for months at a time. He was also occupied as patron of the charitable foundation that he had set up with his wife. However, in mid-June he got together in a London studio with the legendary Jerry Lee Lewis, in order to record a version of "Rock and Roll" for Jerry's album of duets *Last Man Standing*. Later in the year Page was honoured as a legend himself, and in October he was on hand to receive *Q* magazine's Icon Award, at a ceremony held at the Grosvenor House Hotel in London.

Right: Jimmy Page with his eldest daughter Scarlet.

Touring North America

Opposite: During the autumn of 2005 Robert Plant embarked upon yet another tour of North America with the Strange Sensation, and on 5 October he shared a billing with US rock group Pearl Jam, at Chicago's House of Blues. Organized as a benefit for victims of Hurricane Katrina, which had devastated the US Gulf Coast in August, the event raised as much as $1 million dollars for the American Red Cross and other causes. The Strange Sensation played just a 45 minute set, compared to Pearl Jam's two hours, but as Pearl Jam wound down, Plant joined them onstage to perform Elvis Presley's "Little Sister", Barrett Strong's "Money (That's What I Want)", as well as Led Zeppelin's "Going to California", "Fool in the Rain" and "Thank You", before taking up a guitar to close with Neil Young's "Rockin' in the Free World".

Right: The following month Plant and the Strange Sensation were back in Europe, and in December they began the final leg of their tour with a show at London's Hammersmith Palais.

Polar Music Prize

Opposite and right: On 26 May 2006 the surviving members of Led Zeppelin were reunited once again, although on this occasion it was not to perform, but to collect Sweden's prestigious Polar Music Prize, awarded by The Royal Swedish Academy of Music and the Stig Anderson Music Award Foundation, in recognition of exceptional musical achievement. During the ceremony, which was held at the Stockholm Concert Hall, Led Zeppelin were acknowledged by Deep Purple co-founder John Lord as one of the great pioneering groups in rock music and Plant recalled the recording of *In Through the Out Door*, which had taken place in the Swedish capital in late 1978, at ABBA's state-of-the-art Polar Studios. Swedish rockers The Soundtrack of Our Lives performed a handful of Zeppelin tracks, including "Kashmir" and "Whole Lotta Love", before the awards were handed out to Page, Plant and Jones by King Carl XVI Gustaf. Zoe Bonham was also in attendance, collecting the award on behalf of her late father.

Cornbury Festival

Opposite: Robert Plant, London, July 2006. Following the trip to Sweden Plant performed at New York's Beacon Theatre on 23 June, where he headlined the Benefit For Arthur Lee, which raised money to help Lee pay the medical expenses that he was incurring as a result of suffering from leukaemia. Backed by (former Mott the Hoople frontman) Ian Hunter's band, Plant performed a set that included songs by both Led Zeppelin and Arthur Lee & Love. A week later Plant performed at the opening night of the 40th Montreux Jazz Festival, which paid tribute to Atlantic Records and Ahmet Ertegun, and featured a host of stars, including Steve Winwood, Stevie Nicks, Ben E. King and Solomon Burke. Jimmy Page had also been due to attend, but was reportedly forced to back out due to ill health. Following the show, Plant continued to tour Europe with the Strange Sensation, and on 10 July they appeared at Somerset House in London as part of its series of summer concerts.

Above: Plant performs at Cornbury, July 2006.

UK
MUSIC
HALL
OF
FAME

UK Music Hall of Fame

Opposite: On 14 November 2006, Led Zeppelin were inducted into the UK Music Hall of Fame at Alexandra Palace in London, along with others, including James Brown, Brian Wilson, Rod Stewart and Sir George Martin. Zeppelin were inducted by Queen's Roger Taylor and Australian rock band Wolfmother performed "Communication Breakdown" as a tribute. The ceremony was transmitted live on BBC Radio 2, with televised highlights being broadcast two days later on Channel 4. Robert Plant and John Paul Jones opted not to attend the event, leaving Jimmy Page to collect the award on the band's behalf.

Right: Having made just a handful of live appearances in 2005 and 2006, in early 2007 John Paul Jones returned to the stage, performing at Merlefest in North Carolina in April and at the Syd Barrett Tribute Show at the Barbican, London, in May. The following month he attended the Bonnaroo Festival in Tennessee (pictured), where he took to the stage with several acts, including Uncle Earl, Gillian Welch, Ben Harper and Gov't Mule.

Back together again: O2 Arena 2007

Opposite and above: During the summer of 2007 Plant continued to tour with the Strange Sensation, while Jones was performing in Europe with Robyn Hitchcock. However, rumours began to circulate that Led Zeppelin were planning a one-off performance as a tribute to Ahmet Ertegun, who had died the previous December. In fact, Page, Plant, Jones and Jason Bonham had got together to rehearse in early June, and by September the rumours were confirmed, with the announcement that Led Zeppelin would perform a full two-hour set at London's O2 Arena on 26 November. In a curious echo of earlier days, the show had to be rescheduled when Page broke a finger, but this only seemed to heighten the anticipation, with the media hype building to fever pitch by the time Led Zeppelin exploded onto the stage on 10 December. For Plant, who had always been the most resistant to such reunions, the event may have represented an opportunity to put the disappointments of Live Aid and the Atlantic performances behind him, if not to lay Led Zeppelin to rest once and for all, but if anything, the concert seemed only to whet the appetites of the press and public, and Plant readily admitted that he'd also enjoyed the experience.

Mothership

Opposite: Jimmy Page attends a press conference at Tokyo's Park Hyatt Hotel to announce the imminent release of *Mothership*. In late 2007, to coincide with their reunion, Led Zeppelin issued re-mastered editions of *The Song Remains the Same* on both CD and DVD, as well as the new compilation album, *Mothership*, which was made available on CD and vinyl, and also in a deluxe edition, accompanied by a DVD. The LP would peak at number four in the UK and seven in the US, but top the charts in both Norway and New Zealand.

Above: John Paul Jones with Dave Grohl, Los Angeles, 2008. On 10 February 2008, John Paul Jones was present at the 50th Annual Grammy Awards in Los Angeles, where he took to the stage with the Foo Fighters for their performance of "The Pretender". Rather than playing bass or keyboards, however, on this occasion Jones acted as conductor to the accompanying orchestra, for which he had also supplied the musical arrangement. Later in the year, both Jones and Page would join the Foo Fighters for an encore of "Rock and Roll" and "Ramble On" at London's Wembley Stadium.

Plant and Krauss

Above: Robert Plant and Alison Krauss onstage at the 39th Annual New Orleans Jazz and Heritage Festival, 25 April 2008. Having first performed together at a Leadbelly tribute concert in 2004, in 2007 Plant and Krauss got together with producer T-Bone Burnett to collaborate on the album *Raising Sand*. Featuring covers of songs by such artists as Tom Waits, Gene Clark, Milton Campbell, and the Everly Brothers, as well as a reworking of Page and Plant's "Please Read the Letter", the LP was highly acclaimed and hugely successful, reaching number two on both sides of the Atlantic after its release in October 2007. The following spring Plant and Krauss embarked on their first tour together, performing a series of dates in the US in April, before heading to Britain and Europe the following month.

Opposite: The European leg of the tour concluded on 22 May with a performance at Wembley Arena.

Best pop collaboration

Above: In February 2008, Robert Plant and Alison Krauss won the Grammy Award for Best Pop Collaboration with Vocals, with the first single to be released from their *Raising Sand* LP, "Gone, Gone, Gone (Done Moved On)", which had originally been written and recorded by the Everly Brothers in 1964. Later in the year, Plant attended the CMT Awards in Nashville, Tennessee, where the video for the single won the Wide Open Country Video of the Year.

Opposite: On 16 June it was left to Jimmy Page and John Paul Jones to attend the Mojo Awards ceremony at The Brewery in the East End of London, where they collected the award for Best Live Act on behalf of Led Zeppelin, for their reunion performance at the O2 Arena. Four days later, Page was awarded an honourary doctorate for his services to the music industry by the University of Surrey.

MOJO
MOJO HONOURS LIST

Olympic performance

Above and opposite: To mark the handover of the Olympic Games to London, Jimmy Page and *X Factor* winner Leona Lewis performed a brand new arrangement of Led Zeppelin's "Whole Lotta Love", at the closing ceremony of the 2008 Summer Olympics in Beijing. Accompanied by England football star David Beckham, who kicked a ball into the crowd below, Page and Lewis delivered the song from the top of a converted red double-decker bus, in front of a an audience of over 90,000 at Beijing's National Stadium. Broadcast around the world, the ceremony was thought to have been witnessed by an estimated audience of almost two billion.

It Might Get loud

Opposite: In early September, Jimmy Page attended the Toronto Film Festival, where the documentary *It Might Get Loud* received its world première. Co-produced by Page and Davis Guggenheim, the director of *An Inconvenient Truth*, the film explores the history of the electric guitar, through an examination of the careers of U2's the Edge, Jack White of the White Stripes and the Raconteurs, and Page himself. The film also features the three guitarists performing together, and includes a rendition of the traditional blues composition "In My Time of Dying", which Led Zeppelin had previously recorded as the closing track of their sixth studio album *Physical Graffiti*. During the festival Page, Jack White and the Edge attended a press conference to discuss the making of the movie.

Right: Around the same time, Robert Plant and Alison Krauss attended the Mercury Music Prize ceremony at the Grosvenor House Hotel in London, having been nominated for their folk-infused album, *Raising Sand*.

GQ
dunhill
LONDON
GQ MEN OF THE YEAR 2008
Led Zeppelin

Outstanding Achievement

Opposite: On 3 September 2008 Jimmy Page, Robert Plant and John Paul Jones made a rare group appearance at an awards ceremony, when they attended *GQ* magazine's Men of the Year Awards at London's Royal Opera House, where they were presented with the award for Outstanding Achievement. Other musicians in attendance included the Foo Fighter's Dave Grohl, Bobby Gillespie of Primal Scream, Mark Ronson and Elton John.

Right: Robert Plant performing with Alison Krauss at the Austin City Limits Music Festival in Texas, 27 September 2008. In the autumn, while Plant and Alison Krauss were performing in the US, rumours once again began to emerge that Led Zeppelin were considering a tour. Plant denied the stories, stating that he had no plans to reform the group, being content with his current musical partnership with Alison Krauss, but just days later, it was reported that Page, Jones and Jason Bonham had been auditioning vocalists with a view to touring without the original Zeppelin frontman.

In early 2009 however, it was announced that Page had abandoned the idea of touring without Plant, and in February the singer had further cause to his celebrate his partnership with Alison Krauss when the pair swept the boards at the 51st Grammys, winning five awards, including Album of the Year for *Raising Sand*.

Chronology

1944

Jan 9th James Patrick Page born in Heston, Middlesex

1946

Jan 3rd John Baldwin (John Paul Jones) born in Sidcup, Kent

1948

May 31st John Henry Bonham born in Redditch Worcestershire

Aug 20th Robert Anthony Plant born in West Bromwich, Staffordshire

1957

Page is given his first guitar by his parents

1958

Page appears on ITV's Search for the Stars programme, aged 14

1960

Page performs with beat poet Royston Ellis and joins Red E Lewis and the Red Caps

Jones begins playing bass at boarding school, going on to play with his father's band

1961

Page joins Neil Christian and the Crusaders

1962

Nov Page appears on the Crusaders' single, "The Road to Love", produced by Joe Meek. After a stint of touring with the band he will enrol at Sutton Art College

1963

Feb Page appears on Jet Harris and Tony Meehan's number one hit single, "Diamonds"

Jones joins Jet Harris and Tony Meehan's group

Bonham receives his first drum kit from his father

1964

As musical director for Andrew Loog Oldham, Jones begins to establish himself as a leading session musician and arranger, working on sessions by the Rolling Stones and Nico, amongst others. In Apr he will release the instrumental single, "Baja"/"A Foggy Day in Vietnam"

Page performs on numerous hit records, establishing himself as one of the UK's leading session guitarists

Plant performs with Andy Long and the Original Jaymen, The Black Snake Moan, and The Crawling King Snakes

John Bonham joins Terry Webb and the Spiders, also recording "She's a Mod" with the Senators

1965

Bonham marries his girlfriend, Pat Phillips

Feb Page releases solo single, "She Just Satisfies"/"Keep Moving"

1966

Bonham and Plant perform together in The Crawling King Snakes.

Jones becomes musical director for Mickie Most, arranging sessions for Herman's Hermits, Lulu, and Donovan

Page arranges and performs on "Beck's Bolero", featuring Nicky Hopkins, Keith Moon and Jones, prompting him to consider forming a new supergroup. Moon reportedly suggests the name "Lead Zeppelin"

Jun Page joins the Yardbirds on bass, quickly switching to play dual lead guitar alongside Jeff Beck

Jul 15th Bonham's son Jason is born

Oct Plant sings lead vocals on Listen's "You Better Run"/"Everybody's Gonna Say"

Nov Beck departs from the Yardbirds, leaving Page as the sole lead guitarist

Dec Jones works as arranger for the Yardbirds' "Little Games"

1967

Peter Grant becomes manager of the Yardbirds

Plant and Bonham perform together in the Band of Joy

Jones marries his girlfriend Maureen

Mar Plant releases solo single, "Our Song"/ "Laughing, Crying, Laughing"

Sept Plant releases solo single "Long Time Coming"/"I've Got a Secret"

1968

Having begun to perform regular dates in London, The Band of Joy support US singer Tim Rose as he begins his British tour

Page and the Yardbirds perform "I'm Confused" for a John Peel radio session. Based on a composition by Jake Holmes, the song will later become Led Zeppelin's "Dazed and Confused"

Apr Page and Jones record together on Donovan's "Hurdy Gurdy Man". Having heard rumours that Page is considering forming a new band, Jones asks Jimmy to bear him in mind for the position of bassist

May Band of Joy split; Bonham joins Tim Rose's backing group for another UK tour, Plant begins recording with "The Father of British Blues", Alexis Korner

Jun Jim McCarty and Keith Relf leave the Yardbirds. Page features on the sessions for Joe Cocker's "With A Little Help From My Friends"

Jul 7th final Yardbirds performance, at Luton Technical College

Aug having seen Plant perform with the band Hobstweedle in Birmingham, Page invites the singer to his Pangbourne home, where he will ask him to join the New Yardbirds. Plant recommends Bonham as drummer

Aug Page, Plant, Jones and Bonham gather for the first time to rehearse in London. The following month they will back PJ Proby, as the New Yardbirds, during his recording of "Three Week Hero"

Sept 7th still billed as the Yardbirds, the group begin a short tour of Scandinavia, with their debut performance in Gladsaxe, Denmark

Oct 4th the line-up make their British debut in Newcastle

Oct 11th Plant plays harmonica for a BBC session with Alexis Korner and Steve Miller

Oct 25th the band perform as Led Zeppelin for the first time, at Surrey University

Oct Led Zeppelin record their eponymous debut album at Olympic Studios, London

Nov 9th Plant marries girlfriend Maureen. Led Zeppelin perform at the Roundhouse in Camden. John Lee Hooker also features on the bill

Nov 13th Atlantic announce their signing of Led Zeppelin, the first rock act to be contracted to the parent label

Nov 21st Plant's daughter Carmen is born

Dec 26th after further UK dates, Led Zeppelin begin their first North American tour at the Denver Coliseum, Colorado

1969

Jan 12th debut album *Led Zeppelin* is released in the US

Feb 15th last date of first North American tour at Thee Image Club, Miami, Florida. Debut album enters US top 40

Feb 24th Led Zeppelin perform at the Lafayette Club, Wolverhampton for Pat Bonham's 21st birthday

Mar–Apr further UK and European dates

Mar 10th "Good Times Bad Times"/ "Communication Breakdown" is released as a single in the US. It will peak at number 80

Mar 17th performance recorded in Copenhagen, Denmark, for Danish television

Mar 19th recording session for BBC radio

Mar 21st Led Zeppelin's sole live UK television performance, playing "Communication Breakdown" on the BBC's How Late It Is

Mar 25th filmed for "Supershow" in Staines, which also features Eric Clapton, Jack Bruce, Buddy Miles, Buddy Guy and Stephen Stills

Mar 28th UK release of *Led Zeppelin I*

Apr 18th Led Zeppelin begin their second North American tour at the New York University Jazz Festival

May tour continues, interspersed with recording sessions at various US studios. Debut album enters US top 10

May 31st US tour ends at Fillmore East, New York

Jun recording sessions for second LP and also for BBC Radio at various London locations

Jun 13th first proper UK tour begins in Birmingham

Jun 19th performance recorded for French television in Paris

Jun 28th Led Zeppelin perform in front of an estimated 12,000 fans at the Bath Festival of Blues, which also features John Mayall, Fleetwood Mac and Ten Years After

Jun 29th UK tour concludes at the Royal Albert Hall, London, where Led Zeppelin headline the first night of the Pop Proms, supported by The Liverpool Scene and Mick Abraham's Blodwyn Pig

Jul 5th third North American tour commences at the Atlanta Pop Festival, Georgia, before an estimated audience of 40,000. This tour will take in numerous festivals, including the Newport Jazz Festival, the Schaefer Music Festival in Central Park, the Seattle Pop Festival, and the Singer Bowl Music Festival in New York

Aug album sessions take place in New York and Los Angeles

Aug 31st tour closes at the Texas International Pop Festival

Sept Page and Bonham feature on Screaming Lord Sutch's "Lord Sutch and Heavy Friends", which Page also produces.

Oct European and UK dates

Oct 12th Led Zeppelin perform at London's Lyceum Theatre, for which they reportedly receive the then highest fee for a one-off performance by a British group.

Oct 17th Led Zeppelin begin their 4th North American tour with a performance at New York's Carnegie Hall, becoming the first rock band to play the venue since the Beatles and the Rolling Stones in 1964

Oct 22nd release of *Led Zeppelin II*. Advance orders already top 400,000

Nov 7th "Whole Lotta Love"/"Living Loving Maid (She's Just A Woman)" is issued as a US single

Nov 8th tour concludes at the Winterland Ballroom, San Francisco

Nov first recording sessions for *Led Zeppelin III* at Olympic Sound Studios, London

Dec 5th UK release of "Whole Lotta Love" halted by Peter Grant

Dec 6th Led Zeppelin play a one-off show in Paris, France, which also features The Pretty Things

Dec 11th Led Zeppelin presented with gold and platinum discs by the Parliamentary secretary to the Board of State at the Savoy Hotel, London. Page receives minor injuries in a car accident en route to the ceremony

Dec 27th *Led Zeppelin II* knocks the Beatles' Abbey Road from the top of the US charts, where it will remain for seven weeks

1970

Jan "Whole Lotta Love" reaches number 4 on the US *Billboard* chart

Jan 7th a series of 8 UK dates begins in Birmingham

Jan 9th Page celebrates his 26th birthday performing with Led Zeppelin at the Royal Albert Hall, where he meets French model Charlotte Martin. The show is professionally filmed for a prospective documentary and features Jones playing Hammond organ as well as bass. John Lennon, Eric Clapton and Jeff Beck reportedly attend

Feb 7th *Led Zeppelin II* tops the UK chart. Edinburgh concert is re-scheduled for the 17th after Plant receives minor injuries in a car accident

Feb 23rd European tour begins in Helsinki, Finland

Feb 26th Led Zeppelin interviewed for Swedish television

Feb 28th Led Zeppelin perform in Copenhagen as "The Nobs", following threats of legal action by Eva Von Zeppelin

Mar 12th European tour comes to an end in Dusseldorf, Germany

Mar 21st Led Zeppelin begin their 5th North American tour in Vancouver, Canada, their first without a support act. Page's guitar goes missing en route to Canada

Mar 28th Led Zeppelin appear on the Beat Club television show,

Apr 5th problems with PA system and rowdy audience in Baltimore

Apr 13th Led Zeppelin set a new attendance record for the Montreal Forum, performing to a sell-out crowd of 17,500 fans

Apr 17th Led Zeppelin are honoured with the keys to the city ahead of their performance in Memphis. That night Plant struggles to tame a rowdy audience, whilst backstage, manager Peter Grant is reportedly threatened with a gun by the local promoter

Apr 18th Phoenix show is cut short as Plant is taken ill

Apr 19th final show of the tour due to take place in Las Vegas is cancelled as Plant loses his voice

Apr 26th Page appears on Julie Felix's BBC television show, performing "White Summer"/"Black Mountain Side"

Apr–May Page and Plant retreat to Bron-yr-Aur cottage, near Machynlleth, Wales, in order to write material for their next LP

May Led Zeppelin convene at Headley Grange in Hampshire to record

May/Jun recording moves to Olympic Sound Studios, London

Jun 22nd Led Zeppelin perform in Iceland, inspiring the composition of the Viking-themed "Immigrant Song"

Jun 28th Led Zeppelin headline the Bath Festival at the West Showground, Shepton Mallet, following performances by Frank Zappa and the Mothers of Invention, and Jefferson Airplane. Audience estimates range from 150,000 to 250,000. "Immigrant Song" receives its live debut

Jul 16th Led Zeppelin perform in Cologne, the first of four consecutive nights in Germany

Jul recording sessions take place at the newly-opened Island Studios, London

Aug 15th originally scheduled to begin ten days earlier in Cincinnati, Led Zeppelin launch their 6th North American tour at the Yale Bowl, New Haven, Connecticut

Aug final mixing of *Led Zeppelin III* completed at Ardent Studios, Memphis, Tennessee

Sept 18th Page and Plant interviewed at a press conference in New York

Sept 19th tour concludes with two performances at the Madison Square Garden, where Plant pays tribute to Jimmy Hendrix, who had died the previous day

Sept 27th Led Zeppelin end the Beatles' eight year reign as "Top Group" in the *Melody Maker* annual readers' poll

Oct 5th US release of *Led Zeppelin III*. With advance orders nearing 1 million, the album instantly attains gold status

Oct 16th Led Zeppelin are honoured for their contribution to the British export economy at another gold disc presentation

Oct 23rd UK release of *Led Zeppelin III*

Oct 31st *Led Zeppelin III* tops the US album chart

Nov 5th "Immigrant Song"/"Hey Hey What Can I Do" is released as a single in the US

Nov 7th *Led Zeppelin III* tops the UK album chart for three weeks. It will return to the top spot for a further week from the 12th Dec

Dec recording sessions at Island Studios and Headley Grange

1971

Jan recording continues at Headley Grange

Jan 30th "Immigrant Song" peaks at number 16 in the US

Feb recording at Island Studios and Olympic Sound Studios, London. Engineer Andy Johns then mixed the LP at Sunset Sound, Los Angeles

Feb 14th Led Zeppelin voted "world's top band" at the *Disc and Music Echo* awards, London

Mar 5th over five months since their last performance, Led Zeppelin launch their spring tour in Belfast, where "Stairway to Heaven" receives its live debut

Mar 23rd UK club tour concludes at London's Marquee

Mar 24th birth of Jimmy Page and Charlotte Martin's daughter, Scarlet

Apr 1st Led Zeppelin recorded live at the Paris Cinema, London, for John Peel's *In Concert* radio show

May 3rd "Misty Mountain Hop" receives its live debut at a performance in Copenhagen, whilst "Four Sticks" finds its way into a live set for the only time

Jun 29th John Bonham jams with various acts at the Rock Revival Show, Birmingham, England

Jul 5th as fans clash with riot police in Milan, Italy, Led Zeppelin are forced to abandon their performance mid-set. Tear gas was deployed, forcing the band from the stage, which was then overrun and destroyed

Aug 7th and 8th two shows at the Montreux Casino, Switzerland. Four months later, the Casino would be burnt to the ground during a Frank Zappa concert, inspiring Deep Purple's "Smoke On The Water"

Aug 19th Led Zeppelin's 7th North American tour begins in Vancouver, Canada. Overcrowding leads to several injuries amongst fans and a partial stage collapse

Aug 20th Plant's 23rd birthday arrives as he gives an interview to Journalist Rick McGrath following the show in Vancouver

Sept 3rd front of stage collapses under the weight of fans at Madison Square Garden

Sept 17th American tour draws to an end with the second of two performances in Honolulu, Hawaii

Sept 23rd & 24th Led Zeppelin play their first shows in Japan at the Nippon Budokan, Tokyo. "Immigrant Song" is at the top of the Japanese chart

Sept 25th Led Zeppelin spend the evening jamming with local musicians in a club in Kyoto

Sept 27th Taiikukan for victims of the World War II atomic bombing. Led Zeppelin were awarded Peace Medals and the the city's Civil Charter

Sept 29th the short Japanese tour concludes at the Festival Hall in Osaka. Page and Plant go on to visit Hong Kong, Thailand and India

Oct the Sunset Sound tapes being useless, Page and engineer Glyn Johns produce the final mix of the fourth album in London

Nov 8th Led Zeppelin's untitled fourth album is released. It will go on to become one of the biggest-selling albums in history

Nov 11th Led Zeppelin begin UK tour in Newcastle

Nov 20th & 21st Led Zeppelin play two nights at London's Wembley Empire Pool. Entitled "Electric Magic", the shows feature circus performers and support acts

Nov 23rd Bonham's brother Mick joins the band on stage in Preston to play congas during "Whole Lotta Love"

Dec 2nd "Black Dog"/"Misty Mountain Hop" is released as single in the US and Australia, where it will peak at numbers 15 and 11 respectively

Dec 4th Led Zeppelin's 4th LP peaks at number 1 on the UK album chart. It will reach number two the US

Dec 9th show in Coventry is briefly disrupted by an IRA bomb scare

Dec 21st UK tour closes in Salisbury

1972

Bonham buys Old Hyde Farm, Cutnall Green, Worcestershire

Jan rehearsals and recording at Page's home studio, Sussex and Olympic Sound Studios, London

Feb 6th Plant and Bonham jam with Fairport Convention at the Lafayette Club, Wolverhampton

Feb 13th Led Zeppelin refused entry to Singapore on account of their long hair, forcing the cancellation of a performance due the following day

Feb 16th tour of Australia and New Zealand begins in Perth. The concert is marred by rioting, as numerous fans attempt to storm the Subiaco Oval without paying. That night Led Zeppelin are subject to a drugs raid at their hotel

Feb 21st "Rock and Roll"/"Four Sticks" issued as single in US

Feb 22nd Led Zeppelin interviewed by Germaine Greer in Sydney

Feb 29th tour concludes in Brisbane, following which Page and Plant travel to Bombay, India, where they will record with local musicians, including members of the Bombay Symphony Orchestra

Apr 12th Robert and Maureen Plant's son, Karac is born

Apr–May recording sessions at Mick Jagger's Stargroves estate, Berkshire, and Olympic and Island Studios, London

May 27th warm-up performance in Amsterdam, Holland

May 28th warm-up performance in Brussels, Belgium, in front of a particularly rowdy audience

Jun 6th Led Zeppelin begin their 8th North American tour at Cobo Hall, Detroit. Thanks to manager Peter Grant, the band commands an unprecedented 90 per cent of box office receipts

Jun recording and mixing for 5th LP at Electric Lady Studios, New York

Jun 18th following rioting at the Rolling Stones Vancouver concert a few days earlier, Led Zeppelin's scheduled Vancouver show is replaced by an extra date in Seattle

Jun 25th Led Zeppelin perform at the L.A. Forum. The show will later feature on the live album *How the West Was Won*, along with recordings from Long Beach Arena on the 27th. Page meets 14-year-old model Lori maddox

Jun 26th Plant interviewed for DJ Wolfman radio show, Los Angeles

Jun 28th tour comes to an end at the Tucson Community Centre, Arizona

Oct 2nd Led Zeppelin begin their 2nd Japanese tour at the Budokan Hall, Tokyo

Oct 10th last night of Japanese tour, Kaikan Hall, Kyoto

Oct rehearsals at the Rainbow Theatre, London

Oct 28th & 29th two dates at the Montreux Pavillion, Switzerland

Nov Page visits the Rolling Stones in Jamaica, where he participates in a jam session

Nov 10th 110,000 tickets for forthcoming UK tour sell out within four hours

Nov 30th Led Zeppelin's biggest UK tour begins at Newcastle City Hall

Dec 23rd first leg of UK tour comes to an end with the second of two shows at London's Alexandra Palace

1973

Jan 2nd second leg of UK tour begins in Sheffield. Plant is suffering from flu, having hitch-hiked to the gig with Bonham after their car broke down

Jan 16th Led Zeppelin play in front of a very reserved audience, including several local officials, at Kings Hall, Aberystwyth

Jan 31st UK tour concludes in Preston

Feb 16th release of 5th LP, *Houses of the Holy*, postponed due to problems with sleeve design

Mar 2nd European tour begins in Copenhagen, Denmark

Mar 20th a preview of "No Quarter" is broadcast by Bob Harris on BBC 2's Old Grey Whistle Test

Mar 28th release of *Houses of the Holy* LP

Mar 27th Led Zeppelin and entourage arrested in France but are soon released

Mar 29th & 31st concerts in Lille and Marseille are cancelled following trouble at shows in Lyon and Nancy

Apr 2nd European tour concludes with the second of two nights at the Palais Des Sports, Paris, France

Apr rehearsals at Old Street Film Studios and Shepperton Studios, London

Apr 14th *Houses of the Holy* reaches the top of the UK chart

May 4th Led Zeppelin begin the first leg of their mammoth ninth North American tour at the Atlanta Stadium, setting an attendance record for Georgia by attracting a crowd of around 49,200

May 5th second show of the tour at Tampa Stadium, Florida, attracts an audience of some 56,800, breaking the Beatles' attendance record for a single performance, set at Shea Stadium in 1965

May 12th *Houses of the Holy* tops the *Billboard* album chart in the US, displacing Elvis Presley's *Aloha from Hawaii* Via Satellite

May 14th Jones Jams with Atlantic Records executives Phil Carson and Jerry Greenberg at Cosimo's Studios, New Orleans

May 23rd Led Zeppelin are reportedly threatened at gunpoint by the owner of a ranch where they are staying in Texas

May 24th US release of single "Over The Hills and Far Away"/"Dancing Days"

May 28th Page sprains finger on a mesh fence at San Diego airport

May 31st Bonham celebrates his 25th birthday with a performance at the L.A. Forum. Bonham later throws George Harrison and his wife Pattie into a swimming pool

Jun 2nd Page and Plant interviewed for Radio One in San Francisco. Led Zeppelin headline an all day festival at Kezar Stadium, which also features Roy Harper, The Tubes, and Lee Michaels. Bonham douses promoter Bill Graham with water after the show

Jun 3rd the first leg of the North American tour closes at the Forum in Los Angeles

During Jun break, Plant buys a working

sheep farm on the Welsh coast, whilst Page outbids David Bowie to buy "Tower House" from actor Richard Harris

Jul 6th Led Zeppelin begin the second leg of their summer tour in Chicago. During their break, tour manager Richard Cole has secured the use of luxury private jet, "the Starship"

Jul 18th performance in Vancouver is cut short when Plant is taken ill, having reportedly been spiked backstage during Bonham's "Moby Dick" solo

Jul 23rd Joe Massot and his film crew begin shooting footage of the band at their performance in Baltimore

Jul 27th the first of three consecutive nights at Madison Square Garden, which bring the North American tour to a close. The band are reportedly paid over $400,000 for the shows, which are filmed for *The Song Remains the Same*

Jul 29th on the final night of the tour, Led Zeppelin are robbed of $203,000 from a safe deposit box at the Drake Hotel, New York. The following morning Peter Grant is arrested after punching a photographer at the hotel.

Aug Led Zeppelin return to England. Plant heads to Morocco to holiday

Aug 11th a reward of $10,000 is offered for the return of the money stolen in New York

Sept 17th US release of single, "D'yer Mak'er"/ "The Crunge"

Sept 29th Plant is awarded "Top Male Singer" at the Melody Maker awards, London

Oct Joe Massot begins fiming individual sequences for Led Zeppelin's movie, *The Song Remains the Same*

Octr–Dec Jones produces Madeline Bell's LP *Comin' Atcha* at Morgan Studios, London, and Dormouse Studios at his Sussex home

Nov recording sessions for next album at Headley Grange, as well as Page's recordings for Kenneth Anger's Lucifer Rising, probably made at Boleskin House, former residence of Alistair Crowley

Dec 3rd Page performs with Roy Harper at London's Royal Albert Hall

Dec 6th Jones performs with Madeline Bell on BBC TV's *Colour My Soul*

Dec 12th having recently produced Madeline Bell's *Comin' Atcha* LP, Jones plays bass with the singer for BBC television. He is considering leaving Led Zeppelin at this time, on account of their punishing touring schedule

Dec 29th "D'yer Mak'er"/"The Crunge" peaks at number 20 in the US

1974

Jan recording sessions resume at Headley Grange. Peter Grant negotiates a new deal with Atlantic, announcing that future releases will be issued on Led Zeppelin's own label

Feb 1st Jones is interviewed for BBC radio

Feb 14th Page performs with Roy Harper, Keith Moon, Ronnie Lane and Max Middleton as the Intergalactic Elephant Band, at London's Rainbow Theatre. Bonham plays guitar on the final song, whilst Plant closes the show as MC

Apr Bonham appears in Harry Neilson's musical comedy Son of Dracula

May Led Zeppelin and Peter Grant launch their Swan Song record label, signing Maggie Bell and Bad Company, and opening offices in London and New York. The launch is celebrated with parties in New York and Los Angeles

May 11th while in LA, Page, Plant and Bonham watch Elvis perform at the Forum. He acknowledges them during the performance, and they later meet him at his hotel

Jun 15th Bad Company's eponymous debut LP becomes the first Swan Song release

Aug further sequences are filmed for *The Song Remains the Same* at Shepperton Studios, London. Peter Clifton has now replaced Massot as director

Aug 31st Jones joins Dave Gilmour of Pink Floyd alongside Roy Harper at a performance in London's Hyde Park

Sept 1st Page joins Bad Company on stage in Austin, Texas

Sept 14th Page and Bonham join Crosby, Stills, Nash & Young in an jam at an after party held at Quaglinos Restaurant, London

Sept 24th Page joins Bad Company onstage in Central Park, New York

Oct final mixing of *Physical Graffiti* takes place at Olympic Sound Studios, London

Oct 15th Page records "Scarlet" at Island Studios, with Keith Richards, Ron Wood and others. The song is never released

Oct 31st a lavish party is held at Chislehurst Caves, Kent, to celebrate the release of the Pretty Things' *Silk Torpedo*, Swan Song's first UK album release

Nov 26th rehearsals at the Livewire Theatre, London

Dec 19th Jones and Page join Bad Company on Stage at the Rainbow Theatre, London

1975

John and Pat Bonham's daughter Zoe is born

Jan 11th Led Zeppelin play a warm-up show in Rotterdam, Holland, their first live performance since Madison Square Garden, Jul 1973

Jan 12th warm-up show in Brussels, Belgium. Plant is interviewed by the BBC's Bob Harris before the show

Jan 13th Page breaks his finger in a train door at London's Victoria Station

Jan 17th having arrived in the US, the set is revised to accommodate Page's injury. In the UK, Plant's interview is broadcast on *The Old Grey Whistle Test*

Jan 18th Led Zeppelin's 10th North American tour begins at the Met Centre, Minneapolis

Jan 20th Plant suffers from flu, badly affecting his voice for the first leg of the tour

Feb 3rd with Page's finger recovering, "Dazed and Confused" is returned to the set at Madison Square Garden, New York. Writer William S. Burroughs attends, after which he and Page conduct an interview for *Crawdaddy!* magazine

Feb 4th scheduled Boston show is replaced with an extra performance in Uniondale, New York, after fans ransack the Boston Garden ahead of the gig

Feb 6th Bonham is introduced as Karen Carpenter at Led Zeppelin's Montreal Show, Playboy magazine having just voted her Best Rock Drummer of 1975

Feb 8th Plant reportedly strikes a security guard with his mic stand during a performance at the Spectrum, Philadelphia

Feb 13th Ronnie Wood joins Led Zeppelin onstage at the Nassau Coliseum, Uniondale, New York

Feb 16th first leg of tour concludes with a re-scheduled show at the Missouri Arena, St. Louis. Page and Plant holiday in Dominica

Feb 21st previews of "Houses Of The Holy" and "Trampled Underfoot" are broadcast on The Old Grey Whistle Test

Feb 22nd Alan Freeman previews "Custard Pie", "Down By The Seaside", "Night Flight", "The Wanton Song" and "Sick Again" on his Radio One Rock Show

Feb 24th release of double LP, *Physical Graffiti*. The album enters the *Billboard* chart at number 3

Feb 27th tour resumes in Houston, Texas

Mar Led Zeppelin meet Bob Dylan in LA, Maggie Bell releases Suicide Sal, featuring contributions from Page and Bonham

Mar 8th Florida show is cancelled

Mar 15th *Physical Graffiti* tops UK chart. Tickets for forthcoming Earls Court shows sell out in four hours

Mar 19th Plant interviewed for radio in Vancouver

Mar 22nd *Physical Graffiti* reaches the top of the US charts, where it will remain for six weeks

Mar 27th North American tour ends with the last of three shows at the LA Forum. The set runs for almost three and a half hours, and includes a 46 minute rendition of "Dazed and Confused"

Mar 29th Led Zeppelin make history, as all six of their albums are simultaneously on the *Billboard* album chart

Apr 2 US single release of "Trampled Under Foot"/"Black Country Woman"

Apr Page, Plant and Grant visit New York on business. Page does some mixing for *The Song Remains The Same* at Electric Lady Studios. Plant is interviewed by Wolfman Jack for the Midnight Special television show

Apr 19th two further dates are added to the Earls Court shows

Apr–May lighting tests and rehearsals at Earls Court

May 10th limited edition of 5,000 copies of "Trampled Under Foot"/"Black Country Woman" pressed in UK but not released

May 17th the first of the five Earls Court Arena shows in London. "Trampled Under Foot"/"Black Country Woman" peaks at number 38 in the US

May 25th final performance at Earls Court arena. During the run, some 85,000 fans have attended the shows

May–Jul Robert and Maureen Plant holiday in Morocco, where they will meet Page in Jun, before rejoining the band in Montreux, Switzerland

Jun Page's interview with William S. Burroughs is printed in *Crawdaddy* magazine

Aug Robert, Maureen and their children holiday in Rhodes, Greece, with Page, Charlotte Martin and their daughter Scarlet

Aug 3rd Page heads to Sicily to visit a property that once belonged to Alistair Crowley

Aug 4th Plant and his family are seriously injured in a car accident in Rhodes. Tour manager Richard Cole charters a plane to fly them back to Britain for treatment, but as a tax exile, Plant must fly on to Jersey to recuperate

Sept with touring plans shelved, Plant relocates to Malibu, and is joined by Page

Sept 27th Page and Bonham collect an unprecedented seven first-place *Melody Maker* awards in London, including International Band Of The Year, International Live Act Of The Year, and best album for *Physical Graffiti*

Oct Led Zeppelin rehearse and record at SIR studios, Los Angeles.Page is still wheelchair-bound

Nov 9th – 27th Led Zeppelin record and mix their seventh album, *Presence*, at Musicland Studios, Munich, Germany

Dec 10th Led Zeppelin guest with former Tornados pianist Norman Hale at Behan's, Jersey

1976

Jan Led Zeppelin head to New York, where their movie *The Song Remains the Same* is being finalized. Bonham reportedly interrupts a Deep Purple show to advertise Led Zeppelin's forthcoming album and to insult guitarist Tommy Bolin

Feb Led Zeppelin win eight awards in the NME reader's poll, including Best Vocal Group, Best Singer, Best Drummer and Best Guitarist, as well as Best Producer for Jimmy page

Mar Page is interviewed for Alan Freeman's *Radio One Rock Show*

Mar 31st 7th album *Presence* is released in the US, where the LP immediately attains platinum status, becoming the first album to achieve over 1 million sales on advance orders alone

Apr 3rd Alan Freeman plays *Presence* in its entirety on Radio One

Apr 5th UK release of *Presence*. In Britain the album achieves gold status on the day of release

Apr 6th Bob Harris presents "Achilles Last Stand" on The Old Grey Whistle Test

Apr 24th *Presence* tops the UK album chart

May 23rd Page and Plant join Bad Company on stage at the LA Forum. Bonham attends, but does not play on account of an injured hand

May 26th Page and Plant reportedly insult actor Telly Savalas on their return flight to the UK

May 27th Jones joins the Pretty Things onstage at the Marquee, London

Jun 18th release of "Candy Store Rock"/"Royal Orleans" as a single in US. It will peak at number 50

Jun 19th Plant attends The West Coast Rock Show, Ninian Park, Cardiff, where acts include Bob Marley, Eric Burdon, Country Joe & The Fish, Gloria Jones and The Pretty Things

Jul Dave Edmunds is signed to Swan Song

Aug mixing sessions for *The Song Remains the Same* at Trident Studios, London

Sept Kenneth Anger fires Page from the Lucifer Rising project, the guitarist and producer having supplied just over 20 minutes of music as the result of three years work

Sept 12th Page and Bonham record a drum track at Mountain Studios, Montreux, Switzerland, which will later appear on Coda

Sept 28th *The Song Remains the Same* soundtrack is issued in the US as a double LP.

Oct 5th The Old Grey Whistle Test presents an exclusive film clip of "Black Dog" from *The Song Remains the Same*

Oct 9th tickets go on sale for London screenings of Led Zeppelin's movie

Oct 16th Alan Freeman previews "No Quarter" and "Whole Lotta Love" from the *The Song Remains the Same* soundtrack, on His Radio 1 Rock Show

Oct 20th world premiere of Led Zeppelin's movie, *The Song Remains the Same* in New York. Showco in Dallas supply a quadraphonic sound system for the event

Oct 22nd *The Song Remains the Same* LP receives its UK release. The movie also receives its West Coast premiere in Los Angeles

Oct 23rd excerpts of *The Song Remains the Same* are shown on Don Kirshner's US television show

Nov 2nd Plant and Peter Grant are interviewed on The Old Grey Whistle Test

Nov 3rd *The Song Remains the Same* soundtrack is certified gold in the UK. It will go on to top the album chart ten days later, whilst it will stall at number two in the US

Nov 4th *The Song Remains the Same* receives its European premiere at two London Cinemas. It will open nationally three days later

Nov–Dec Led Zeppelin begin preparations for their next US tour, rehearsing live arrangements of "Achilles Last Stand" at EEZE Hire Studios, London

1977

Jan further rehearsals at Emerson Lake and Palmer's Manticore Studio's in London

Jan 13th Page and Plant watch the Damned perform in London. Bonham accompanies Plant to a Damned gig four days later

Feb 5th Led Zeppelin announce plans for a world tour, to begin in the US before the end of the month

Apr 1st originally scheduled to begin in Fort Worth, Led Zeppelin's 11th North American Tour begins late in Dallas, Texas, with Plant recovering from laryngitis

Apr 9th third consecutive show at the Chicago Stadium is cut short and rescheduled for the following night when Page collapses, supposedly from food poisoning

Apr 10th Page takes to the stage in Chicago in Nazi uniform

Apr 19th around 70 fans are arrested after would-be gate-crashers attempt to break into the show at the Riverfront Coliseum, Cincinnati

Apr 20th a boy falls from the stadium at the band's second show in Cincinnati. He will later die in hospital

Apr 25th Led Zeppelin temporarily leave the stage in Kentucky after Page's guitar is struck by a bottle thrown from the crowd

Apr 30th the first leg of the tour ends in front of a record-breaking audience of 76,229 at the Pontiac Silverdome, Michigan

May Led Zeppelin return to England, although Page visits Egypt

May 12th Led Zeppelin honoured for their contribution to music at an Ivor Novello luncheon in London

May 18th North American tour resumes in Birmingham, Alabama

May 21st several arrests are made following vandalism by fans after the show in Houston

May 22nd Bad Company's Mick Ralphs joins the band on stage for an encore in Fort Worth, Texas

Jun 3rd show at Tampa Stadium is cancelled because of rain, leading to rioting

Jun 7th the first of a six night run at Madison Square Garden, New York

Jun 9th Page is interviewed for a New York radio broadcast

Jun 27th the second leg of the tour ends with the last of six performances at the LA Forum. Four days earlier Keith Moon had joined the band onstage at the venue

Jun 28th Led Zeppelin return to the UK for another break

Jul 17th The third and final leg of the 1977 North American tour begins in Seattle

Jul 23rd John Bonham, Peter Grant, Richard Cole and security guard John Bindon are involved in a backstage brawl with members of Bill Graham's staff at the Oakland Coliseum

Jul 24th the second show at the Oakland Coliseum goes ahead as planned, but the following day Bonham, Grant, Cole and Bindon are charged with assault

Jul 26th Plant, Bonham and Cole travel to New Orleans, where Plant learns of the sudden death of his son, Karac in England. The remainder of the tour is immediately cancelled and they return to England

Aug 14th Page and Ron Wood join a charity jam session at the Half Moon, Plumpton

Sept rumours abound that Led Zeppelin are to split. Bonham breaks three ribs in a car accident near his home

Sept 8th Page participates in a jam session with Phil Carson, Bill Kinsley and Carl Simmons at the annual Warner Elektra Atlantic record company sales conference at the Metropole Hotel, Brighton

Oct 3rd Page appears on Nicky Horne's Capitol Radio show, where he attempts to dispel rumours of a split

1978

Feb Plant records backing vocals and produces a session with punk band Dansette Damage at the Old Smithy Studios, Kempsey, Worcestershire. He is credited as both the Wolverhampton Wanderer' and 'Uncle Bob'

Feb 16th the assault charges against Bonham, Grant, Cole and Bindon are heard in California. All incur fines and suspended sentences

May Led Zeppelin convene at Clearwell Castle in the Forest of Dean, Gloucestershire, in order to rehearse, record and discuss the future of the band

Jun Plant makes a guest appearance on children's television show *Tiswas*, along with Rainbow drummer Cozy Powell

Jul Plant joins local band Melvin's Marauders on stage at the Wolverly Memorial Hall, Kidderminster

Aug Plant appears on stage with Phil Carson and Dr Feelgood at Club Amnesia, San Raphael, Ibiza

Sept 15th Page, Plant and Jones attend Richard Cole and Simon Kirke's joint wedding reception in London

Sept 16th Plant joins Dave Edmunds on stage at Birmingham Town Hall

Oct 3rd Bonham and Jones join Paul McCartney and Wings' Rockestra session at Abbey Road, which features Dave Gilmour, Hank Marvin, Kenny Jones, Ronnie Lane, Gary Brooker, Tony Ashton, and Pete Townshend

Oct Led Zeppelin return to EZEE Hire Studios, London, for rehearsals

Nov 1st Plant and Jones attend a rock raffle at the Golden Lion, Fulham, London

Nov 6th Led Zeppelin head for Abba's Polar Studios in Stockholm, Sweden, to begin work on a new album

Nov 24th Bonham makes an appearance with a local band at Stourport Civic Hall

Dec initial recordings are completed before Christmas. Page works on mixing some of the tracks at his home studio in Plumpton

1979

Jan 21st Robert and Maureen's son Logan is born

Feb mixing sessions take Place at Polar Studios, Stockholm

Mar 26th Plant joins Bad Company on stage at the Birmingham Odeon Theatre

Apr 3rd Page, Plant and Bonham join Bad Company on stage at the Birmingham Odeon Theatre

May press reports circulate that Led Zeppelin will soon return to the stage

May 8th Plant and Jones attend Dave Edmunds wedding reception

May 16th Plant appears with Melvin's Marauders at the Stourbridge Wine Bar in the West Midlands

May 22nd Led Zeppelin announce their intention to headline an outdoor show at Knebworth Park, Hertfordshire

Jun 3rd tickets go on sale for Knebworth

Jun 9th BBC Radio One broadcasts an interview with Robert Plant conducted backstage at a Dave Edmunds performance

Jun 26th Led Zeppelin attend a Rockpile gig in Hammersmith

Jul 4th the band begin rehearsals at Bray Studios, Berkshire, where new lighting effects are tested and some video footage is taken. A second Knebworth date is announced due to ticket demand

Jul 19th the line-up for Knebworth is confirmed

Jul 23rd & 24th two warm up shows at the Falkoner Theatre, Copenhagen, Denmark. "Hot Dog" and "In The Evening" are performed live for the first time

Aug 3rd Led Zeppelin soundcheck at Knebworth

Aug 4th Led Zeppelin's first Knebworth Festival show. Support acts include Fairport Convention, Chas and Dave, Commander Cody, Southside Johnny and The Asbury Jukes, and Todd Rundgren's Utopia

Aug 11th second Knebworth show. Keith Richards and Ron Woods New Barbarians play in place of Fairport Convention. It will prove to be Led Zeppelin's final UK appearance

Aug 15th Led Zeppelin issue their 8th studio album, *In Through The Out Door*. It will top the charts on both sides of the Atlantic within a week of its release

Oct 27th Led Zeppelin's entire catalogue of nine LPs is to be found on the *Billboard* Top 200 in the same week, a feat unmatched by any other group or artist

Nov 28th Plant, Jones, Bonham and Peter Grant attend the Melody Maker Awards at London's Waldorf Hotel, where they receive several awards, including Best Group, Best Male Vocalist and Best Album

Dec 2nd Page attends Paul McCartney and Wings' performance in Brighton. Paul, Linda and Denny Laine stay at Page's home

Dec 7th "Fool In The Rain"/"Hot Dog" issued as US single

Dec 29th Plant, Jones and Bonham participate in the Concert For The People Of Kampuchea at the Hammersmith Odeon, London. Plant appears with Dave Edmund's Rockpile, whilst Jones and Bonham join the all-star line up, performing the "Rockestra Theme", "Let It Be" and "Lucille"

1980

Jan 16th "Fool In The Rain"/"Hot Dog" reaches number 21 in the US. K-Tel and Swan Song launch The Summit charity compilation album in London. Plant attends the reception, along with Eric Clapton and Phil Lynott

3rd Feb Plant joins Dave Edmunds' Rockpile on stage at the Top Rank Ballroom, Birmingham

Mar 4th Bonham films a live interview with Billy Connolly for the Tyne Tees show Alright Now

Apr 27th Led Zeppelin begin rehearsals at the Rainbow Theatre, London

May 5th rehearsals continue at London's New Victoria Theatre

May 11th European tour dates are confirmed for Germany, Belgium, Holland, Austria and Switzerland

May 18th rehearsals move to Shepperton Studios, concluding on Jun 6th

Jun 17th Led Zeppelin launch their tour in Dortmund, Germany. It will prove to be their last

Jun 27th the band's Nuremburg show is cut short after three songs as Bonham is apparently suffering from food poisoning

Jun 30th Phil Carson joins Led Zeppelin on stage for an encore in Frankfurt

Jul 1st Page joins Santana for a rendition of "Shake Your Money Maker" in Frankfurt, Germany

Jul 5th Simon Kirke of Bad Company joins Led Zeppelin onstage to close the show in Munich

Jul 7th Led Zeppelin close the European tour with a final show in Berlin. It is the last ever performance featuring the original line-up of Robert Plant, Jimmy Page, John Paul Jones and John Bonham

Aug Plant, Jones and Bonham take a holiday. Page moves to Windsor, having purchased Old Mill House from actor Michael Caine

Sept 11th Peter Grant announces plans for an extensive North American tour, scheduled to take place from Oct 17th to Nov 15th

Sept 21st US box offices report unprecedented demand for tickets

Sept 24th rehearsals take place at Bray Studios, Berkshire, following which the group head to Page's Windsor home

Sept 25th having been drinking heavily the previous night, John Bonham is discovered unconscious in a spare bedroom at Page's house by Jones and Benji Lefevre. An ambulance is called but efforts to revive him prove futile, and he is pronounced dead at the scene

Sept 26th the police announce that there are no suspicious circumstances surrounding Bonham's death

Sept 27th the planned North American tour is cancelled as tributes pour in from around the globe

Oct 7th following an inquest, Bonham's death is ruled to have been an accident

Oct 10th John Bonham's funeral takes place at Rushock, Worcestershire

Oct 18th rumours circulate in the press concerning Bonham's possible replacement

Nov 7th Page, Plant and Jones adjourn to Jersey to discuss Led Zeppelin's future

Dec 4th Led Zeppelin announce that they are to disband in the wake of Bonham's death

1981

Jones establishes a recording studio in Devon

Mar 10th Page joins Jeff Beck on stage at the Hammersmith Odeon

Mar - Jul Plant performs a series of low-key gigs around the UK with the Honeydrippers

Apr Page forms XYZ with Chris Squire and Alan White, but management issues and Plant's reluctance to get involved see the project quickly shelved

Aug Plant begins recording solo material at Rockfield Studios in Wales, with Phil Collins and Cozy Powell on drums

Sept Page writes and records the soundtrack for the movie *Death Wish II* at his home studio

Dec 15th Page, Plant, Jones and Peter Grant attend a charity raffle at the Golden Lion, Fulham, London

Dec 30th Plant performs in Dudley, with John's son, Jason Bonham on drums

1982

Jones begins teaching Electronic Composition at Dartington College of Arts, Devon

Mar Page begins work on a compilation LP consisting of studio outtakes spanning Led Zeppelin's career

May 12th Page and Plant join Foreigner on stage in Munich

Jun 28th release of Plant's first solo album, *Pictures at Eleven*. It rapidly rises to number two on the UK chart and will reach the top 5 in the US

Jul 21st Plant appears the Prince's Trust charity event held at the Dominion Theatre, London. Other guests include Pete Townshend, Jethro Tull, Kate Bush, Phil Collins and Madness

Sept release of Plant's solo single "Burning Down One Side"

Oct Page receives a conditional discharge for possession of cocaine

Nov 19th release of 10th Led Zeppelin album, *Coda*

Nov Jones films a sequence for Paul McCartney's *Give My Regards to Broad Street*

Dec 13th Page joins Plant on stage at the Hammersmith Odeon, London

1983

May 24th Page joins Eric Clapton on stage in Guildford, Surrey

Jul 11th Plant releases his second album, *The Principle of Moments*. It will reach the top ten on both sides of the Atlantic, whilst the single "Big Log" will fall just short of the UK top 10

Aug Robert and Maureen Plant divorce

Aug 20th Plant embarks on his first solo tour in St. Louis, Missouri, concluding in Seattle on Sept 30th

Sept 20th & 21st Page performs "Stairway to Heaven" as part of an all-star charity concert for ARMS (Action Research into Multiple Sclerosis), at the Royal Albert Hall, London

Oct the Swan Song label is dissolved

Nov 22nd Plant launches his UK tour in Glasgow

Nov 28– Page performs in Dallas, San Francisco,

Dec 9 Los Angeles and New York as the ARMS benefit concerts continue in the US

Dec 4th Jones joins Plant on stage in Bristol

Dec 13th Page joins Plant on stage at the Hammersmith Odeon, London

Dec 24th Jason Bonham joins Plant on stage in Birmingham for the last show of his solo tour

1984

Jan 22–Feb 25 Plant tours Australia, New Zealand and Japan

Feb 15th Page jams with Eric Clapton, Charlie Watts, John Entwistle and Louis Bertignac in New York, to celebrate sound engineer Glyn Johns' birthday

Feb 29th Plant's tour ends in Kowloon, Hong kong. Atlantic's Phil Carson joins the stage to play bass

Jun 24th Page appears on stage with Yes in Dortmund, Germany

Jul 28th Page and Roy Harper perform together at the Cambidge Folk Festival

Aug Page forms The Firm with Paul Rodgers, Tony Franklin and Chris Slade

Sept Jones records the soundtrack for the Michael Winner movie *Scream for Help*. Page performs on two tracks

Nov 12th Plant releases "The Honeydrippers Vol. One". The EP features Cozy Powell, Phil Collins, Page and Jeff Beck, and will reach the top five in the US

Nov 16th Page and Roy Harper are featured on *The Old Grey Whistle Test*

Nov 29th The Firm begin a European tour in Stockholm, Sweden

Dec 8th & 9th The Firm play two nights at the Hammersmith Odeon

Dec 15th Plant and the Honeydrippers appear on Saturday Night Live. "Sea of Love" from the EP reaches number 3 in the US

1985

Jan Plant releases "Sea of Love" in the UK

Jan 18th Plant and the Honeydrippers play a one-off show in Monmouth, Wales, billed as the Skinnydippers

Feb 11th The Firm release their eponymous debut LP

Feb 28–May 9th The Firm embark on a US tour

Mar 4th Page and Roy Harper release the album, *Whatever Happened to Jugula*

Mar 22nd Jones' soundtrack LP, *Scream for Help* is issued, featuring contributions from Page. Plant releases the single "Pink and Black"

May 18th The Firm begin a series of UK dates

May 20th Plant releases his third solo LP, *Shaken 'n' Stirred*

Jun 10th Plant begins a North American tour

Jul 13th Led Zeppelin reunite for the US Live Aid concert in Philadelphia, with Phil Collins and Tony Thompson on drums

Jul 23rd Page joins Plant on stage in New Jersey

Aug 5th Plant's North American tour closes in New York

Aug 19th Plant issues the single "Little by Little"

Sept 10th Plant performs at Wembley Arena

1986

Page marries Patricia Ecker

Jones produces Ben E. King's 14th studio album, *Save The Last Dance For Me*

Jan Page, Plant and Jones reunite to record and rehearse in Bath, with Tony Thompson on drums.

Feb 3rd The Firm's second album, *Mean Business*, is released in the US

Mar 14th–May 28th The Firm's second US tour

Mar Plant plays a series of dates with The Big Town Playboys

Mar 24th *Mean Business*, is released in the UK

Jul 4th Page appears on stage with the Beach Boys in Washington

Aug 9th Plant appears on stage with Fairport Convention at the Cropredy Festival, Oxfordshire

Nov 9th Page joins Iron Maiden, Brian May and Bad News for a charity performance in London

Dec 19th Page joins Plant on stage for a benefit gig at the Stourport Civic Centre

1987

Jan Page starts work on the solo LP *Outrider* at his home studio. Jason Bonham plays drums, whilst Plant guests on "The Only One"

Mar 2nd Jones joins Ben E. King on stage at the London Palladium

Jul Jones produces The Mission's Children LP

Sept Plant begins recording a new solo album, *Now and Zen*. Page performs on two tracks

Dec 17th Plant performs in Folkstone, Kent with his new band, billed as The Band of Joy

Dec 30th The Band of Joy perform at Stourbridge Town Hall

1988

Plant attends the Nordoff-Robbins Music Therapy Foundation's Silver Clef Award and Auction dinner, New York, where he jams with Buckwheat Zydeco, Curt Smith and Neil Young

Jan 18th Plant releases the single "Heaven Knows", featuring Page on guitar

Jan Plant plays three warm-up gigs, in Leicester, Southampton and Colchester

Feb 3rd Plant performs at London's Marquee

Feb 29th Plant's *Now and Zen* LP is released. It will reach the top ten on both sides of the Atlantic

Mar 16th Plant begins a UK tour in Newport, South Wales

Mar 27th Jones joins The Mission on stage at London's Astoria

Apr 11th Plant releases the single "Tall Cool One", featuring Jimmy Page. It will reach number 25 in the US

Apr 17th on the final night of Plant's UK tour, he is joined by Page at the Hammersmith Odeon. They perform an encore that includes Led Zeppelin's "Trampled Under Foot", "Misty Mountain Hop" and "Rock and Roll"

Apr 26th Page's son James Patrick Page Jr. is born

May Plant embarks upon an extensive North American tour that will run until the end of Jul. His sets will include several Led Zeppelin compositions

May 14th Led Zeppelin reunite to perform at Atlantic Records' 40th anniversary celebrations, Madison Square Garden, New York. Jason Bonham plays drums

Jun 20th release of Page's solo album, *Outrider*

Jul 23rd Jones performs with Julie Felix in Fife, Scotland

Sept Page tours the US with Jason Bonham on drums

1989

Nov the surviving members of Led Zeppelin perform at Carmen Plant's 21st birthday celebrations

Dec 23rd Plant performs a charity show in Kidderminster with local band Out of the Blue

1990

Jan rumours abound that Led Zeppelin are to reform for a summer tour

Jan 10th Page joins Bon Jovi on stage at the Hammersmith Odeon

Mar 19th Plant releases his *Manic Nirvana* LP. As with his previous solo efforts it will reach the top 20 on both sides of the Atlantic

Apr 28th Page, Plant and Jones perform a Led Zeppelin set with Jason Bonham at his wedding reception in Bewdley, Worcestershire

May 1st–Jun 7th Plant embarks upon a two-month tour of British and European cities

Jun 30th Page and Plant perform at the Silver Clef charity concert, Knebworth

Jul 5th Plant launches another extensive North American tour in Albany, New York

Aug 18th Page jams with Aerosmith at Donnington's Monsters of Rock Festival.

Two days later they will do the same at London's Marquee Club

Oct 15th UK release of Remasters boxed set. It will reach the UK top 10

Oct 29th release of *Led Zeppelin (Boxed Set I)*

Nov 26th Plant's North American tour closes in Muskogee, Oklahoma

Dec 7th Plant performs in Athens, Greece

Dec 12th–16th Plant plays a handful of UK shows, taking in Newcastle, Manchester, Wolverhampton and Newport

1991

Jones establishes a 32 track studio near Bath

Jan 8th–10th Plant performs three shows at the Town & Country Club, London

Jan 18th Jones performs with vocal group Red Byrd at the Queen Elizabeth Hall, London

Mar 23rd & 25th Page performs two shows in New York

May 14 & 29th Page performs two shows in Reno, Nevada

Oct Plant and Jason Bonham perform with local bands The Ripps and Billy & The Bowel Movements at a tribute concert in Kidderminster

Nov & Dec 7th Page performs two shows in Vancouver, Canada

1992

Jones performs on Peter Gabriel's *Us* LP, provides arrangements for R.E.M.'s *Automatic For The People*, and produces the Butthole Surfers' *Independent Worm Saloon*

Jan 15th Page is in attendance as the Yardbirds are inducted into the Rock and Roll Hall of Fame. He performs at the ceremony alongside Jeff Beck and Eric Clapton

Nov 18th Led Zeppelin are awarded Q magazine's Merit Award at the Park Lane Hotel, London

1993

Mar 15th Page and David Coverdale's *Coverdale-Page* LP is released. It will reach number 4 in the UK, and 5 on the *Billboard* top 200

Apr 28th Plant performs "29 Palms" on the BBC's *Top of the Pops*

May 1st Plant performs in Rome, Italy. Two days later he plays a set for radio station RETE in Milan

May 6th Plant joins Def Leppard onstage in Denmark for an encore

May 14th & 20th Plant performs at the King's Head, Fulham

May 18th Plant records before a live studio audience for the BBC's *Later...With Jules Holland television programme*

May 22nd Plant is interviewed on BBC radio

May 25th Plant releases his *Fate of Nations* album. It will reach number 6 in the UK

May 26th Plant Launches his European tour in Prague, Czechoslovakia

Jul 5th Plant performs an acoustic set for Virgin Radio in London

Jul 16th Plants tour concludes at the Brixton Academy, London, where he is joined on stage by the Black Crowes' Chris Robinson

Sept 2nd Jones performs "Are You Gonna Go My Way" with Lenny kravitz at the MTV Video Music Awards, California

Sept 15–Dec 1st Plant tours North America

Sept 21st release of *Led Zeppelin Box Set II*

Sept 24th release of *The Complete Studio Recordings* boxed set

Dec 5th–23rd Plant performs a series of European dates

1994

Page meets Jimena Gomez-Paratcha, with whom he will found the ABC Trust, a charitable foundation for Brazilian street kids. They will soon begin a romantic relationship

Jan Robert Plant plays a series of dates in South and Central America supporting Aerosmith

Apr 17th Page and Plant perform at the Alexis Korner Memorial Concert in Buxton

Jul Page and Plant begin rehearsals at CTS Studios, Wembley

Aug 9th & 10th accompanied by local musicians, Page and Plant film performances of "Wah Wah", "City Don't Cry" and "Yallah (The Truth Explodes)" in Morocco, for their forthcoming MTV special

Aug 12th Page and Plant are filmed performing "No Quarter" in Snowdonia, Wales

Aug 12th–16th Jones performs with Heart in Seattle, going on to produce their live album *The Road Home*

Aug 17th Page and Plant filmed performing "Gallows Pole", "Nobody's Fault But Mine" and "When The Levee Breaks", in Machynlleth, Wales

Aug 25 & 26th Page and Plant record their unplugged studio session in London, accompanied by Michael Lee, Charlie Jones, Porl Thompson, Najma Akhtar, Jim Sutherland, Nigel Eaton, Ed Shermur, the Egyptian Ensemble and the London Symphony Orchestra

Oct 12th MTV broadcasts Page and Plant's 90 minute *Unledded* special

Oct 14th *No Quarter: Jimmy Page and Robert Plant Unledded* is released as an LP. It will reach the top 10 on both sides of the Atlantic

Oct 19–Dec 12th Jones tours Europe and North America with Diamanda Galas, with whom he will record the album *The Sporting Life*

Nov 11th Page, Plant and the Egyptian Ensemble record a performance for the BBC's *Later... With Jools Holland*

1995

Jan 12th Led Zeppelin are inducted into the Rock and Roll Hall of Fame at New York's Waldorf-Astoria Hotel. The presentation is made by Aerosmith's Steven Tyler and Joe Perry

Jan 16th Page and Patricia Ecker divorce

Jan 30th Led Zeppelin are awarded the Best International Artist Award at the American Music Awards, Los Angeles

Feb 4th Page jams with the Black Crowes in Paris

Feb 26–May 27 Page and Plant tour North America

Mar 21st *Encomium*, a tribute to Led Zeppelin by various artists, is released by Atlantic

Jun 6–Jul 9th Page and Plant perform a series of European dates

Jun 25th Page and Plant perform at the Glastonbury Festival

Jul 12th–26th Page and Plant tour Britain and Ireland

Jul 25th Peter Grant attends Page and Plant's performance at Wembley Arena

Sept 23–Oct 27th Page and Plant tour Mexico and North America

Nov 21st Peter Grant suffers a fatal heart attack whilst driving to his Sussex home with his son, Warren

Dec 4th Page, Plant and Jones are amongst those in attendance at Peter Grant's funeral, held in Hellingly, East Sussex

1996

Jones establishes a studio in London and begins recording his first solo album

Jan 20th–27th Page and Plant perform in Brazil, Chile and Argentina

Feb 5th–29th Page and Plant tour Japan and Australia

Nov 30th Led Zeppelin are recognized with a Lifetime Achievement Award at the Channel V music awards in Mumbai, India. Page and Plant appear with Queen's Roger Taylor

1997

Page and Plant begin work on new LP

Billboard and the Record Industry Association of America (RIAA) report that Led Zeppelin are the second highest-selling act of all time, with ten of their albums certified multi-platinum

Jan the Rock and Roll Hall of Fame inducts "Dazed and Confused", "Rock and Roll", "Stairway to Heaven" and "Whole Lotta Love" into their 500 Songs That Shaped Rock and Roll

May 29th Led Zeppelin are awarded a Lifetime Achievement Award at the Ivor Novello ceremony, held at London's Grosvenor Hotel

Jun Page's daughter Zophia-Jade is born

Sept "Whole Lotta Love" is released as an edited CD single in the UK, becoming Led Zeppelin's first British single release. The song will peak at number 21

Nov 17th release of BBC *Sessions* double CD

Dec 7th Page and Plant perform with Charlie Jones and Michael Lee at a charity event at London's Café de Paris

1998

Mar 5th Page and Plant are filmed for the BBC's *Later...With Jools Holland* in London

Apr 21st Page and Plant release the album *Walking Into Clarksdale,* which was engineered by Steve Albini. It will reach number 3 in the UK and number 8 in the US

May VH1 rank Led Zeppelin at number four on their "Greatest Artists of Rock & Roll" poll

May 9th Page joins Puff Daddy on Saturday Night Live in New York to perform "Come With Me"

May 19–Jul 19th Page and Plant tour North America

Aug Page and Plant make a handful of European performances, including a headlining slot at the Reading Festival, England. Puff Daddy's single "Come With Me", featuring Jimmy Page, hits the charts. It will reach numbers 1 and 2 in the US and UK respectively

Sept 5–Oct 2nd Page and Plant tour North America

Oct 30–Dec 3rd Page and Plant perform in Britain and Europe

Dec 10th Page and Plant perform at an Amnesty International Concert in Paris

1999

According to the RIAA, Led Zeppelin become the third act in history to be awarded four or more Diamond albums

Jan Page's son Asher Josan is born

Feb Page and Plant receive a Grammy Award for Best Hard Rock Performance for their single "Most High"

Mar 16th in New York Page and Jones collect an RIAA Diamond Award on behalf of Led Zeppelin for album sales in excess of 10 million

Jun 16th Page performs an instrumental version of "Dazed and Confused" at a charity function in London

Jun 27th Page performs with the Black Crowes, Guy Pratt, Michael Lee, Steven Tyler and Joe Perry at a charity event at London's Café de Paris

Jul 23–Dec 23rd Plant plays a series of low-key dates in England and Wales with his folk-rock band the Priory of Brion

Sept Jones releases his debut instrumental solo LP *Zooma*

Oct 2–Nov 22nd Jones tours Europe and the US

Oct 9th Page attends NetAid in New York, where he performs with both Puff Daddy and the Black Crowes

Oct 12th–14th Page performs 3 nights at the Roseland Ballroom in New York, alongside the Black Crowes

Oct 16th Page and the Black Crowes are joined onstage by Aerosmith's Joe Perry at the Centrum in Worcester, Massachusetts

Oct 18th & 19th Page performs with the Black Crowes at the Greek Theatre, Los Angeles, resulting in the LP *Live at The Greek*

Nov 23rd release of *Early Days: The Best of Led Zeppelin Volume One*

Dec 7th–10th Jones plays three nights in Japan

2000

Jan four Led Zeppelin compositions, "Rock and Roll", "Kashmir", "Whole Lotta Love" and "Stairway to Heaven" feature in VH1's countdown of "100 Greatest Rock Songs"

Feb 8–Dec 21st Plant tours Britain and Europe with the Priory of Brion

Feb 29th Page and the Black Crowes release Live at The Greek

Mar 9–Apr 2nd Jones tours North America

Mar 21st release of compilation album *Latter Days: The Best of Led Zeppelin Volume Two*

Apr 14th & 15th Jones performs two shows in Italy

Jun 24–Aug 12th Page plays a series of US dates with the Black Crowes. The tour is scheduled to run until Oct, before heading to Britain and Europe, but is cancelled after Page injures his back. The Black Crowes will later sue Lloyds of London for failing to honour their insurance agreement

Nov VH1 list Led Zeppelin as number one on their "Greatest Artists of Hard Rock" countdown

Nov 17th the John Paul Jones Orchestra opens for King Crimson at The House of Blues, Las Vegas, Nevada

2001

Jones releases his second solo album *The Thunderthief*

Jan VH1 include *Led Zeppelin I, Led Zeppelin II* and *Physical Graffiti* amongst their "100 Greatest Albums" listings

Apr 22–May 2nd Plant plays a series of Scandinavian dates with his new band, the Strange Sensation

May 2–Jun 6th Plant plays a series of dates in North America

Plant performs at the Gwardia Stadium, Warsaw, Poland

Aug 14th Plant and the Strange Sensation play further European dates

Jul 7th Page and Plant perform at the Montreux Festival, Switzerland, where Led Zeppelin's "Candy Store Rock" is performed live for the first time

Nov 8th Jimmy Page performs Led Zeppelin's "Thank You" at the MTV Europe

Awards, with Limp Bizkit's Fred Durst and Puddle of Mudd's Wes Scantlin

Nov 9–Dec 14th The John Paul Jones Orchestra tours North America in support of King Crimson

2002

Jan 27th Jones performs a charity concert in Salford with Julie Felix. Bill Wyman & The Rhythm Kings featuring Georgie Fame, Steve Harley, Kiki Dee and Roy Harper also appear

Feb 5th Plant and the Strange Sensation perform in Bristol

Feb 9th Plant performs at the Teenage Charity Concert at London's Royal Albert Hall

Apr 12th Jones plays another benefit show with Julie Felix, at Borders Bookshop, London

May 22–Nov 14th Plant and the Strange Sensation undertake an extensive tour of Britain, Europe and North America. In Jul and Aug they share a bill with the Who for several of their US dates

Jul 16th Plant releases the LP *Dreamland*, featuring his new group the Strange Sensation

Aug 22nd Plant attends Cadillac's centennial celebrations in Detroit

Nov 19th release of the combined compilation album *Early Days and Latter* Days. It will reach number 11 in the UK

Dec 31st Plant features on the BBC's *Later... With Jools Holland* New Years Eve show, performing "Let The Boogie Woogie Roll"

2003

Jan 8th Plant performs at "Festival in the Desert", Mali, with Strange Sensation guitarist Justin Adams

Feb 28th Plant performs for BBC TV's *ReCovered*

Mar 2nd Jones performs at Robyn Hitchcock's 50th birthday party at the Queen Elizabeth Hall, London

Mar 20th Plant performs for BBC TV's *Live Floor Show*

Apr 26th Plant appears at the Ole Blues Festival, Bergen, Norway

May 26th release of Led Zeppelin DVD. It will become the biggest selling music DVD of all time

May 27th release of triple live album *How the West Was Won*. It will top the US album charts and reach the top 5 in the UK

May 28 and 29th Page, Plant and Jones record interviews for NBC's *Tonight* and *Today* shows in New York

Jun 17–Aug 23rd Plant plays a series of UK and European dates, including several festivals

Aug 29 & Sept 1 Jones performs in Japan as part of "Guitar Wars" with Nuno Bettencourt, Paul Gilbert and Steve Hackett

Nov 4th Plant releases a collection of his solo recordings entitled *Sixty Six to Timbuktu*

Dec 6th Plant performs on Jools Holland's Radio 2 show

Dec 11th Plant performs at the Nobel Peace Prize Concert, Oslo, Norway

2004

Jones produces the Datsuns' *Outta Sight Outta Mind* LP

Jan 17th Jones performs at the Barbican, London, as part of John Cage's "Musicircus"

Mar 13th Jones joins Steve Hackett on stage for an encore at London's Shepherds Bush Empire. Plant joins an impromptu jam with Vanilla Fudge at the Rock Café 2000, Stourbridge

May 1st Jones joins the "Midnight Jam" at Merlefest, Wilkesboro, North Carolina

Jul 27–Aug 22nd Jones tours the US with the Mutual Admiration Society

Aug 23rd Jimmy Page inaugurates the London Walk of Fame outside the Virgin Megastore, Piccadilly

Oct 29th Jones makes his first appearance at the Festival Mandolines de Lunel in France. He will perform there again in 2005 and 2006

Nov 7th Plant performs at the Rock And Roll Hall Of Fame 9th annual master music series Tribute To Leadbelly in Cleveland, Ohio, with Justin Adams, Alison Krauss, The Cleveland Four, the Tarbox Ramblers and Los Lobos

2005

Jones performs on the Foo Fighters' LP *In Your Honour*

Feb 13th Led Zeppelin receive a Grammy Lifetime Achievement Award in Los Angeles

Febr 19th & 20th Plant performs in Bristol at a benefit in aid of victims of the 2004 Indian Ocean tsunami

Mar 11–Apr 27th Plant and the Strange Sensation tour the US, UK and Europe

Apr 25th international release of Plant and the Strange Sensation's *Mighty ReArranger* LP, it will be issued in the UK and US in May, where it will reach numbers 4 and 22 respectively

Jun 3rd & 4th Plant and the Strange Sensation perform on the Isle of Man

Jun 11th Plant and the Strange Sensation perform at Nelson Mandela's 46664 Arctic concert in Tromso, Norway

Jun 15th Page contributes to the Jerry Lee Lewis album *Last Man Standing*, performing a blistering solo for Lewis' version of "Rock and Roll"

Jun 15–Jul 31st Plant and the Strange Sensation tour North America

Jun 17th Jones performs at the Barbican London with the Merce Cunningham Dance Company

Aug 20th & 21st Plant and the Strange Sensation perform at the V Festivals, in Chelmsford and Staffordshire. Five days later they will appear at Rock En Seine in Paris

Sept 5th Jones joins Nickel Creek for an encore in London

Sept 10–Oct 6th Plant and the Strange Sensation tour North America

Sept 28th Jones performs at the Talking Bob Dylan Blues tribute concert at London's Barbican

Oct 5th Plant performs with Pearl Jam for a benefit in aid of victims of Hurricane Katrina

Oct 10th Jimmy Page receives an "Icon Award" at the Q Awards, at London's Grosvenor House Hotel

Oct 27th–Dec 13 Plant and the Strange Sensation tour Britain and Europe

Dec 14th Page is presented with an OBE

2006

Jan 1st Plant and the Strange Sensation perform on Andy Kershaw's BBC Radio show

Jan 31st Jones performs with Robyn Hitchcock, Scott McCaughey, Peter Buck and Bill Rieflin at the Three Kings pub, London

Feb 26th Plant performs with the Thrift Store All Stars in California

Mar 10th–Apr 7th Plant and the Strange Sensation tour Europe

May 4th Plant and the Strange Sensation perform at a memorial concert for Ali Farka Touré

May 22nd Led Zeppelin are awarded the Polar Music Prize in Stockholm, Sweden

Jun 23rd Plant performs at an Arthur Lee Benefit Concert, New York

Jun 30th Plant performs at the Montreux Jazz Festival, Switzerland

Jul 1–Aug 13th Plant and the Strange Sensation play a series of British and European dates

Sept 14th Plant performs at the Sunflower Jam Benefit, London, raising funds for cancer charity, The Sam Buxton Sunflower Healing Trust

Oct release of Plant's DVD, *Soundstage: Robert Plant and the Strange Sensation, recorded live in Chicago in Sept 2005*

Nov 14th Led Zeppelin are inducted into the UK Music Hall of Fame

Nov 21st release of Plant's box set, *Nine Lives*

Dec 23rd Plant performs at Kidderminster Town Hall with the Return of the Honeydrippers

2007

Feb 14th Plant performs in Dudley, with the Return of the Honeydrippers

Mar 10th Plant and the Strange Sensation headline the Desert Rock Festival, Dubai

Apr 7th Plant performs with Tinariwen in Paris

Apr 26th–28th Jones participates in Merlefest, Wilkesboro, North Carolina

May 10th Jones performs at the Syd Barrett Tribute Show at London's Barbican

Jun 15th–17th Jones performs at the Bonnaroo Festival, Tennessee, taking to the stage with several acts, including Uncle Earl, Gillian Welch, Ben Harper and Gov't Mule

Jun 22–Aug 1st Plant tours Europe with the Strange Sensation

Jul 30–Aug 4th Jones performs with Robyn Hitchcock in Italy and Norway

Aug 18th Plant and the Strange Sensation headline the Green Man Festival, Powys, Mid Wales

Sept 12th following persistent rumours, the NME confirms that Led Zeppelin are to reform for a one-off show at the O2 Arena, London

Sept 14th Jones performs with Robyn Hitchcock at the End of the Road Festival, Dorset

Sept 24th release of *Goin' Home: A Tribute To Fats Domino*, which featured two tracks from Robert Plant

Oct 5th Plant performs at a benefit for the Birmingham Children's Hospital

Oct 23rd Plant and Alison Krauss release their collaborative album *Raising Sand*

Oct 24th Plant performs on NBC's Today Show in New York, with Alison Krauss, T-Bone Burnett, Buddy Miller, Marc Ribot, Jay Bellerose and Dennis Crouch

Oct 30th Plant & Alison Krauss appear on Mark Radcliffe & Stuart Maconie's BBC Radio show

Nov 8th launch of the dedicated Led Zeppelin digital radio channel, XM LED

Nov 13th Led Zeppelin release the compilation album *Mothership*

Nov 20th release of remastered version of *The Song Remains the Same*

Dec 10th Led Zeppelin reunite with Jason Bonham on drums to perform a tribute concert for Ahmet Ertegun at the O2 Arena, London

2008

Jan Plant is reported to have turned down an offer of $200 million to tour with a re-formed Led Zeppelin

Feb 4th Jones performs at BBC Radio 2's Folk Awards

Feb 10th Jones conducts the orchestra performing with the Foo Fighters at the Grammy Awards, Los Angeles

Apr 14th Plant and Alison Kraus win the Wide Open Country Video of the Year for "Gone, Gone, Gone (Done Moved On)", at the CMT Awards in Nashville, Tennessee

Apr 19th – 26th Plant and Alison Krauss tour the Southern States of the US

Apr 30th Jones performs at Bergenfest, Norway

May 5th–22nd Plant and Alison Krauss tour Britain and Europe

May 9th Plant, Alison Krauss and T-Bone Burnett appear on the BBC's *Later...With Jools Holland*, performing "Gone Gone Gone (Done Moved On)", "Killing The Blues" and "Rich Women"

Jun 2–Jul 19th Plant and Alison Krauss tour North America

Jun 7th Page and Jones join the Foo Fighters on stage for an encore at Wembley Stadium. They perform "Rock and Roll" and "Ramble On"

Jun 20th the University of Surrey awards Page an honorary doctorate for his services to the music industry

Aug 9th Plant joins Kristina Donahue and Fairport Convention at the Cropredy Festival, Oxfordshire, to perform "The Battle of Evermore" in tribute to Sandy Denny

Aug 24th Page performs "Whole Lotta Love" with Leona Lewis at the closing ceremony of the Olympic Games in Beijing

Sept 3rd Led Zeppelin collect the award for Outstanding Achievement at the *GQ* Men of the Year Awards, at London's Royal Opera House

Sept 9th Plant and Alison Krauss attend the Mercury Music Prize as nominees

Sept 5th the documentary *It Might Get Loud*, co-produced by Page and Davis Guggenheim receives its premiere at the Toronto Film Fesival

Sept 23–Oct 5th Plant and Alison Krauss perform a series of US dates

Oct 13th Page, Jones and Jason Bonham are rumoured to be planning a Led Zeppelin tour with singer-songwriter Myles Kennedy replacing Plant

Nov 4th release of 12 disc *Definitive Collection* CD box set

Dec 11th Page performs at the Orange Peel, Asheville, North Carolina, appearing with the Del McCoury Band, Warren Haynes, and Gov't Mule

Dec 12th & 13th Jones performs at the Asheville Civic Centre, North Carolina, appearing with the Allman Brothers Band, Michael Franti, Ben Harper and Gov't Mule, amongst others

2009

Jan the NME reports that Led Zeppelin will not tour again, with or without Plant

Feb 8th Plant and Alison Krauss receive five awards at the 51st annual Grammy Awards, Los Angeles

2010

July Robert Plant embarks on first tour with a new group called Band of Joy.

Sept Plant releases the album *Band of Joy*.

Acknowledgments

All photographs by © Getty Images
except the following
© Atlantic Publishing: 10, 48, 49, 52, 53, 64, 67, 72, 73, 82, 109, 112, 114, 122.